THE GAME OF LIFE

Achieve your dreams and
discover your true self

Louise Presley-Turner

authorHOUSE®

AuthorHouse™ UK Ltd.
500 Avebury Boulevard
Central Milton Keynes, MK9 2BE
www.authorhouse.co.uk
Phone: 08001974150

First published by AuthorHouse 9/3/2009

ISBN: 978-1-4490-1123-9 (sc)

This book is printed on acid-free paper.

Contents

Dedication

To: My beautiful children.

May you achieve every goal and ambition set.
May you live a full and rich life.
May you be blessed with ever-lasting love.
May you appreciate every second of your wonderful life.
But above all, may you always be happy.

I love you.

Acknowledgements

I'd like to acknowledge all those who have had faith in me whilst writing this book. I'd also like to acknowledge all the wonderful authors that have inspired and helped me grow over the years. But above all, I want to thank my husband for all his love and support, I simply wouldn't be where I am today without you!

Introduction

I want more from life than this ...

This book is for you if:

- You wake up each morning feeling tired and apathetic
- You feel let down by life and find yourself saying, 'There must be a better way!'
- You feel time is speeding up and your life is passing you by
- You're completely bored with your current job
- Your relationships aren't what they should be
- You don't like who you have become
- You know you deserve to live a better life
- You long for inner fulfilment and happiness
- You're ready to make some big changes to your life
- You're open and committed to finding a better way to live.

Congratulations! However you have come to be holding this book, whether it was given to you by a friend, family member, colleague or maybe you just liked the cover among all the other hundreds of self-help books on the shelf; whatever the reason, I want you to know that you hold in your hands a book that has the potential to change your life in unimaginable ways. Yes, really!

You have officially taken the first step towards creating the life you know you deserve. You've decided that something's not working, and you're ready to make some changes for the better. This is more than most people do in their entire lifetime.

This book is designed to get you out of your rut and wake you up to whom you really are and what you really want from life. But, before I go on to explain more about its content and how it works, let me share with you my story and the inspiration that led me to write this book.

I remember the turning point in my life like it was only yesterday

Like most of us, I had been busy plodding along, well and truly stuck in the rut, the daily grind of life. Work, sleep, work, sleep ... you know the form. Some days were easier than others, but, on the whole, they all seemed to blend into one, and the years seemed to whizz by at such an alarming speed I was left gasping for air.

I wasn't unhappy, far from it. I realised my blessings and was grateful for them, but I wasn't ecstatic about life either. Something deep inside was missing and I couldn't quite put my finger on it. Externally I had it all: beautiful house in the country; loving and supportive husband; a wonderful daughter; a great lifestyle with lots of holidays. But something was definitely absent. I looked around and it appeared to me that everyone else was in the same rut, doing the same things, so I convinced myself that this was just how life was supposed to be and carried with the status quo.

There were times when I remember looking up at the sky, on a beautiful balmy summer evening, when the last of the day's sunshine was breaking through the clouds and casting wonderful vivid pink and orange rays, and I'd think to myself, 'What is this all about, why are we here?' In those rare moments, without doubt, I knew that the heavens were calling me to dig a little deeper to find the answer to my own question, and I vowed that one day, when I had more time, money, wisdom, and so on, I'd find out. Deep down I knew there was something else

I should be doing with my life, but, of course, like so many of us, I ignored it and carried on filling my life with things that I thought were important until I forgot about my deeper quest for the meaning of life.

Until one day a book landed on my doorstep. This book was like no other I'd come across before, and little did I know at the time that it was to change my life. Having read it, I had unknowingly evoked an almighty power and opened a door into a magical and mystical world of self-discovery, not only for myself but also about questions concerning human existence. The veil was lifted and I was about to reveal the real me!

My journey so far (and I'm still travelling) has been a mixture of highs and lows, but for the first time in my life I have found my calling. I want to help you do the same! By doing so your life will turn a corner, and instead of travelling haphazardly through life, letting the wind take you wherever it will, you can, for the first time, take control and steer yourself towards your chosen destination. Does this sound too good to be true? I know it does, but the truth is right in front of your eyes. It's so simple, yet most of us overlook it because we have never stopped for a second to look and find it!

I think every human being reaches a point in their life when they ask, 'Why?' 'What's my purpose?' 'What's this all about?' Some of us are good at pretending that we don't care, some of us cover this urge with material pleasures, some of us go down the wrong path, and some of us wait until we're on our deathbed before asking these fundamental questions.

I think these questions are part of our blueprint or DNA. We've all thought them at some point, but few of us do more than fleeting contemplation. But we should ask these questions to take us below our surface-thinking, to find the inner fulfilment and happiness that we are all seeking subconsciously. By having the courage and strength to search for the answers, we acquire higher wisdom, an enlightenment that shifts our consciousness and ultimately sets us free.

Are you ready to dig deeper?

What I have rapidly come to realise is that if we don't start to take control of our lives someone else will do it for us!

This book is about taking control: deciding what you want from life, and understanding and implementing new tools and techniques to turn your long-forgotten dream into reality and opening your mind to a whole new way of thinking.

Get ready to make a difference

Now it's all very well buying this book, but, let's be honest, it's not going to do much good if it sits on your bookshelf for the next six months gathering dust and dog hairs. So many people read self-help book after self-help book, and never implement the advice imparted to them. Or some might start using the techniques only to give up a few weeks later because of a lack of tangible results. We're all looking for a quick fix, we all want our fairy godmother to appear from a fluffy white cloud and magically make everything better. But I've got something very important to tell you.

You are your own fairy godmother.

You have a magic wand that can transform your life before your very eyes, but no one has ever bothered to tell you about it. You walk around everyday with magic at your fingertips yet you never use it. How ridiculous is that? Ask yourself this: if what I'm telling you is really true what would you change in your life? Yes, of course you'd magic a million pounds into your bank account … who wouldn't? But, what else would you change? What else would you alter with a wave of your magic wand? Your career? The way you feel about yourself? Your appearance? Your house? Your partner? Your kids? I'm going to show you how to be your own fairy godmother. I'm going to show you where to find your wand and how to start using it. You have all the power you need right now to create whatever it is you want.

I know from experience that the hardest thing about making any kind of change is getting started, but you've done the hard bit – you've made the decision to find a new direction. All you now need to do now is read each chapter of this book and follow any actions I set. I promise that by the time you finish reading this book you'll be eagerly waving your magic wand in all directions and seeing some amazing results.

Some things to consider before you begin your journey

Create time

It's important that you find the time to do the exercises in this book. The exercises aren't the sort of thing you can do while cooking the kid's dinner or doing the ironing. They demand time and thought. Take into account your weekly schedule and work out when you can spend quality time alone. We're not talking hours here, 45 minutes a week will suffice.

Don't rush

We spend our whole lives rushing about. If we're not rushing to work, we're rushing to the shops or for a hair appointment. I want to encourage you to slow down. There are eight chapters in this book, and I suggest that you complete one or two of them each week. But, if it takes longer that's OK too. The key, of course, is not to fall into the trap of procrastination. As long as you are consistently moving forwards, there is no need to rush through each chapter. Absorb the content and move on when you're ready.

Research

Throughout this book I will introduce you to some new and unfamiliar tools and techniques. All the exercises have been created and put together from my own personal experience. They are techniques I have used myself and with my clients, and they have been of huge benefit. But feel free to research other methods; there are many authors out there who will share alternative ideas. Keep your mind open.

Create your support team

When embarking on any personal journey it's always a good idea to get others involved. It's always nice, whether you're feeling a little wobbly or you've made a major breakthrough, to have someone to turn to, maybe your partner, your brother, your best friend or even a good life-coach. A good support team is invaluable and crucial to your success.

My reasons for writing this book

My objective in writing this book was simply to awaken you to who you really are, to give you a deeper awareness of your true origin. When you achieve this you realise that you've spent most of your life sleep-walking – quite literally! This book takes you on a journey of self-discovery; I hope to change your perceptions and open you up to a whole new way of thinking, a whole new reality. And, by doing this you become free to live the life you've always wanted.

I combine both spiritual practices with practical self-help coaching tools to ensure you obtain the maximum benefit. I also encourage you not just to take my word for self-discovery, but to seek those of other teachers as well.

Remember, there is no rush; only we put pressure on ourselves. You cannot plant a daffodil and demand that it blooms overnight, to do so would be unrealistic. It's the same when making changes in our own lives. I encourage you to be patient. I promise if you initiate just a few of the exercises suggested in this book you will notice huge changes in your life.

How this books works

In the next eight chapters we will embark on a journey of self-discovery during which we will cover various topics. You need to read each chapter in turn and complete the exercises as you go along. You might want to read the whole book first and go back over the exercises afterwards. It's up to you. I suggest that you use a special book in which to complete the exercises. You need somewhere you can keep everything together in one place, a cardboard folder will do. You may also wish to make notes in this book.

Here is what we'll cover throughout your journey.

Chapter 1 'Taking stock'

In the first chapter I'll help you to take a clear look at what is currently happening in your life, and at what is making you unhappy and why.

Chapter 2 'What do you *really* want?'

Here we complete one of the most exciting exercises in the book: I will assist you in setting three big life-changing goals that will enhance your life ten-fold.

Chapter 3 'What's going on in your head?'

In Chapter 3 we delve into the dark realms of your mind to discover what you believe about yourself and the world around you, and how this affects your life. I will share with you lots of practical tools that will help you re-programme your mind for success.

Chapter 4 'A new way of thinking'

In this chapter I will introduce you to a new way of viewing the world, and how you may apply this to help create the life of your dreams and achieve anything you set your mind to.

Chapter 5 'Who you really are'

In Chapter 5 we take some time to look at your individual blueprint, and I show you how to build a wonderful life around your values, passions and talents.

Chapter 6 'Beyond your physical self'

I'll be stretching your thinking even further in Chapter 6, as we move beyond the mind and body into the mysterious world of spirit.

Chapter 7 'The real secrets of making it happen'

This chapter is where the real action begins; I give you all the best-kept secrets, tools and techniques to help you make your goals and dreams become real.

Chapter 8 'Facing your fears'

Fear is one of the biggest things that stop us achieving success in life, so, in this final chapter, I will show you how to face your fears head-on to ensure that you never again let fear stop you from achieving what you want.

My job as your personal coach

My job as a personal life coach is unique and very special. My only objective is to ensure that my clients reach their goals, whatever they might be. My role is to give them undivided attention and support. The wonderful thing about my being your life-coach is that I am completely impartial, unbiased and neutral. I have no preconceptions or doubts about your ability to achieve your goals, unlike your family and friends. As much as our families and friends love us, they naturally have their own ideas about what we should and shouldn't, and can and can't, do and this may stop us from moving forwards in life.

I have high expectations for all my clients and I expect them to achieve amazing things while working with me. Just because I am not working with you in person doesn't mean that your journey should be any less powerful or transformational. I want the very best for you, I believe in you and I know you can do it.

Just think … if every human being could live the life they truly wanted, in line with their true self, the world would be a totally magnificent place for each and every one of us.

My job is, first, to help you to become clear about what you actually want from the rest of your life. Many of us don't even plan what we're eating each night never mind what we want from the rest of our lives, so this must be the first step on your journey. I will help you to come face to face with the *real* you for the first time in your life, and I will assist you to move beyond any self-sabotaging behaviours or beliefs that are holding you back. I will help you to adopt a 'Yes, I can' attitude, and we will take on a far more positive outlook to life. And, in true life-coach style, I'll motivate and inspire you to take action. In short, I will give you all the tools and techniques you need to turn your life around.

OK, so sometimes you will curse me or want to throw this book out of the nearest window, but if you stay the distance I guarantee that you a sense of achievement and joy such as you haven't felt since you were a child and had just received a gold star from your teacher.

I get the greatest pleasure out of helping people to achieve their dreams; it's a feeling that money simply cannot buy, and I wouldn't change my job for the world. I love it. So I am here throughout this book (and beyond if you wish) to help you create your perfect life.

Your commitment

Now it's all very well me committing wholeheartedly to you, but what about you making a commitment to yourself. Let's get one thing clear: if you are not committed to the overall journey, both the good and bad, what's the point of starting out? No commitment, no change. If you want big things from life you need to get committed, and now is the time to do so. If you are not dedicated you might as well close this book now and give it to someone else who is. Generally speaking, people who seek out a life coach are completely ready and devoted to making life changes. Just because this is a book and I'm not physically present should not alter your commitment by one iota! You either want change or you don't.

I work with lots of different people, who have all sorts of weird and wonderful goals. Some people achieve rapid results from day one; others are much slower off the mark. Some individuals make enormous changes, others quite small ones. Why so? It all boils down to one thing – *commitment*! The key, of course, is ensuring that you set the right goals from the start; that way your commitment will be unshakeable until the end of your journey.

So ask yourself. On a scale of one to ten (one being 'not bothered', ten being 'totally focused'): 'How committed am I to making some big changes to my life?'

If you answered 'five' or below, I suggest you close this book and come back to it in six months' time. If your answer was 'six' (or above) you are ready to start your life-changing journey.

One last thing: when someone hires me to help them achieve their goals I ask them to sign a coaching agreement. Just as I've outlined above, this agreement states my commitment to my client and what I expect from them as the mentee in return. This way we both know where we stand and there is no ambiguity. So, before we begin, let's do just that.

Our agreement

Coach agreement

I commit to giving you my total dedication, allegiance and focus. I believe in you completely and will support and you encourage you fully.

My signature _____ *Louise* _____

Mentee agreement

I commit to read this book and complete all the exercises outlined, working for a minimum of 45 minutes a week. I am willing to keeping an open mind and try out new ideas and techniques, and I will keep going until I reach my goals.

Your signature _____

OK, I think we're almost ready.

Just one more thing before we begin

Take hold of my hand, I'm right here with you … your journey begins as soon as you turn the page.

Chapter 1

Have you ever stopped to ask directions?

In this chapter I want you to take a snapshot of what is currently happening in your life. Before we can get to the exciting part of setting big life-changing goals it's essential that you look your life squarely in the face and be honest about what is and what is not working. As difficult as this may be, it's imperative that you do this before we move forwards.

No one really wants to admit that they've wasted 20 years of their life in the wrong job, or that they've walked down the aisle with the wrong man, or spent five years training at university only to find out that they're in the wrong career. It's hard to swallow. But, difficult as it is, it's time to be wholeheartedly honest. Most of us spend years putting up with things that make us unhappy, never really getting to the bottom of our unease or understanding why we're feeling unfulfilled. We pretend our life is blissful, even though deep down we know it's not; we smile politely at the world around us, and run round and round our hamster wheel, repeating the same routines day in and day out. We suppress our real feelings until we're totally numb. Then we find ourselves jumping from one job to another one or from one relationship to the next, or we fill our lives with material pleasures that we believe will alleviate our pain and fill the void. None of these things work in the long run. No amount of shoes or DVDs will ever give our soul the inner fulfilment it so desperately seeks. But, because we are anaesthetized, we're oblivious to our own predicament; we just think it's normal. The years pass us by and nothing changes from one year to the next. And the story goes on.

So, how do you know when you're in need of a new direction? Here are some clues.

You wish everyday of the week away. When it's Monday you wish it was Tuesday. When it's Tuesday you wish it was Wednesday. In doing so you never actually live or enjoy the moment.

You watch far too much television, spend too much time on the phone gossiping to friends or searching through social networking websites to see what your mates are up to.

When you get together with your friends all you do is moan about how bad your life is, and then end up feeling totally depressed by the end of the evening. You blame your bad upbringing, your poor education, the country, the economy or whatever for not having the life you want. You're a complete victim.

You're envious of anyone who seems successful, and are quick to point out their faults, or find yourself saying, "Oh well, it's OK for them…'

You drink, smoke or shop too much as a way of making yourself feel better about your life.

You only mix with people who are on your wavelength, as they're the only ones who really do understand what it's like to live your life.

You always wake up feeling groggy and apathetic.

You're always ill, catching every cold or virus going: this is just typical of your luck!

You feel your circumstances are totally out of your control.

Stop that treadmill!

Let's face it most of us are so busy gasping for the air we need just to get through each day that our dreams and goals are put on the back-burner for what seems like an eternity. The days fade into one long arduous week, and before we know it a year has vanished and we've gained yet another wrinkle. We've hardly had time to think about, let alone experience, our dreams and goals. We decide that this is how it must be for everyone because when we look around it appears that everyone is on the same treadmill. Others seem as hard-pressed, prodded, let-down and disappointed by life as we are.

Along comes another year: a time of new beginnings and positive action – a new season of promise and hope. 'This will be the year I change my life,' you hear yourself say. You convince yourself this year will be different, the year you finally lose that weight, start your own business, change career, get out of debt, find your life purpose or bag the man of your dreams. We muster all our ambition and positive energy into making this year the year that catapults us into a brand new exciting life.

But many of us get caught up in the fast pace of modern living, all those hopes and dreams quickly wither away and we're back to running at breakneck speed on our all too familiar treadmill. We resign ourselves to the notion that this is how it is: life's hard and we don't really have any control after all.

Modern living is just like a treadmill, never stopping, never ending. On and on it goes, which is fine if you're heading in the right direction; but if you're not the constant grind over time takes its toll, not only emotionally but on your physical health, too.

In Western society we are conditioned to follow one other around, and I don't mean literally. I mean following past programming from generations gone by – from our family, teachers, friends and culture. In our society it's expected that you leave school, go to university, get your first job, buy your first car, travel, purchase your first house, search frantically for Mr or Mrs Right, have babies and, before we know, it we have created a trap of financial restraints and responsibilities for ourselves. It becomes extremely hard for us to step off or stop that treadmill.

At school I really wanted to be a journalist because I enjoyed writing so much. In my final year I clearly remember having a meeting with my careers teacher to discuss my options. I had a few ideas about what I wanted to do – maybe an air hostess or working in the travel industry in some form or another – but what I really wanted to do was become a writer. I had struggled with most subjects at a school, just about keeping my head above water. But I thoroughly enjoyed English; writing came easily to me and I was actually quite good at it, regularly getting the highest grades in my class. As I sat in front of my teacher, young, naïve and simply looking for some sound guidance to point me in the right direction, her response to my ideas about becoming a writer was, 'You need to be realistic Louise, to be a journalist you need to get "A" grades and then go on to university; have you thought about working with children?' Errrr, no! So there I was, a confused teenager out in the big wide world, what was I going to do with the rest of my life? I had no idea. Thankfully, I didn't follow my teacher's advice. I decided I would find my own direction. Unfortunately I didn't become a journalist, I ended up in a job in advertising, which wasn't a bad thing but it wasn't what I really wanted. It only took 12 years for me to realise this, so I suppose you could say my detour was relatively short in comparison with some. It wasn't until I started my coaching career that I finally put pen to paper.

Regrettably, when it comes to making career choices, schools (and parents for that matter) rarely look at a child's talents, capabilities or passions. They tend to focus on what's logical and where the child would fit in or easily be placed. Most parents are just happy to get their kids into a decent job (any job) and earning a wage. This is understandable, but in doing so they miss something very vital and our children end up on the wrong career path, in occupations that simply aren't right for them. One lady client came to me having spent 20 years working in catering, even though she absolutely hated cooking. She told me that she was very creative, that she loved to sew and regularly designed clothes for herself or made curtains for friends and family. As a child she was excellent at textiles and was told by her teachers at school she had a gift, a natural talent. Her parents rarely took much notice of this and were more concerned that she achieved good grades in both maths and English. When she was 15 her family relocated from Scotland to Manchester, where her father enrolled her on a catering course at the local college. My client had no desire to build a career in the restaurant or catering industry, but it was what her mother had done all her life and she wasn't going to go against her parents' wishes. 'I was only 15, what did I know, I just did what I was told,' she explained to me. When she came to see me, she'd had enough of pretending to be happy, pretending that her life was OK; she wanted change, my client wanted a career that she enjoyed and that came easily to her. She had made a decision to transform her life and subsequently set herself a life-changing goal – to start her own textile business. It only took her 20 years to realise what was wrong and do something about it.

The point I'm trying to make here is: how many of us *really* follow our dreams? How many of us, when we're at such a young and impressionable age, have the courage to go against the grain and do something different. Not many. It's so much easier to follow your dreams when you're young and naïve, and have energy and a passion for life. I'm not saying it impossible as we get older, but it gets harder, that's all. It's no one's fault. We can't blame our parents for our job or the bad relationship we're in. Most parents simply do their best with their beliefs or state of consciousness. They know no different!

I want you to take notice of your treadmill: Are you really happy? Do you have a long lost dream that somehow shifted to the back-burner? Maybe you've been doing the same job for years, it's comfortable but the days drag and you'd much rather be doing something else. Maybe you hop from job to job looking for the right one. Maybe you're stuck in a loveless relationship and too scared to break free. Maybe you're a stay at home mum, bored of being everything to everyone else and having no time for yourself, or maybe, like me, you're content in most areas of your life, but somewhere deep within you is little voice that nudges you every time you buy another lottery ticket in the hope that maybe, just maybe, this time it will be the one that will finally free you forever? Do you hear a little voice that says 'Stop, there is another way'? Do you feel that something is missing, that you should be doing something else with your life? The circumstances don't really matter, but, if you hear that inner call, feel that inner nudge, maybe it is time to start asking some deeper questions.

I wasn't even aware of my own 'rut' because I thought this was normal! Everyone around me was in the same situation and we were all on the same treadmill so I thought that that must be just the way it was. I never once considered that there might be another way. Why should I? We all have a 'comfort zone' inside ourselves where everything is safe, warm and stable. We have rituals and routines that we perform day in and day out and which keep us tucked nicely within our self-created comfort zones.

When was the last time you stopped to see where you were going? Did you check whether it was the right direction? Change is the single most important element in everyone's life and only you can make changes to your life; only you can break free from the 'same old, same old…'!

If you live your life within the confines of your comfort zone you don't give yourself the opportunity to grow, to learn new things, be free, playful and spontaneous, and ultimately to enjoy a fulfilled life.

There's a very simple rule to consider: keep doing the same things and you'll keep getting the same things back. Give yourself permission to expand your awareness and stretch your invisible wings so you may fly a little higher and further to see what else is out there. Who knows what you might find.

The human condition

Here we are: a supposedly intelligent species that can split atoms and fly to the moon. Yet we humans are still running around killing each other, dying of cancer, letting half the world's population starve to death and ruining the planet with all our man-made toxins. Something has gone seriously amiss! This isn't how it's supposed to be, and deep down we all know it! We all need to open our eyes.

We think that by straining, manipulating, controlling and forcing that we will have the ability to change the outward picture of our lives. We spend our whole lives trying to change the people around us, trying to change our current circumstances, working our fingers to the bone just to make ends meet or to buy the material things that we think will bring us happiness. But if this were truly the answer then our world wouldn't be in the mess that it is.

We believe our lives are controlled by our government, our boss, our partner, our neighbour. We honestly believe that we have no control because: 'It's their fault not mine; I'm just the victim.'

There's a world of 'closet sufferers' walking around out there, smiling through their gritted teeth, and who would swear blind that they are happy with their lot. They'll tell you their life is great, that they are totally happy and content. Yet these same people tell you life is hard, it's not fair that you just have to 'put up and shut up' and deal with whatever life throws at you.

I say, 'Rubbish! Life is not for enduring. Far from it, it's about living – living a fulfilled and happy life!'

Closet suffers are just victims, plain and simple, viewing their world from their limited perspective. They honestly believe they have no control.

If I'm honest I, too, was once one of those people, always blaming others for my misfortunes. On a Monday morning in the office you would find me standing over the photocopier, a cup of tea in one hand, a pile of unopened post in the other, gossiping about the events of the weekend or the latest addition to the team. Until my own journey began I was definitely a crowd follower. Partly because I knew no different and partly because it was easier just to fit in.

Here's the truth of the matter. All change must start from within – this is the trick we're all missing!

It's not the government's fault that the economy is in the state it is; it's not your boss's fault that you don't earn enough; it's not your partner's fault that you've grown apart; and it's not your neighbour's fault that their dogs keep barking all day long. I promise you, as long as you keep blaming all those around you, you will remain exactly where you currently are in your life. Nothing will change. YOU need to take responsibility for your life, starting right now.

We live our lives within the rules of society, our families and our culture – we have been told how to sit, how to behave, what to do. Until now, that is! Some people are starting to wake up and are desperately trying to find that missing link in their lives.

There is a revolution afoot. Can you feel it?

Remember, keep doing the same things and you'll keep getting the same things back. Accept that something is not working in your life – let go of the notion that you have no control.

It's time for us to stop being blinkered and insular, and to open our minds to new possibilities. In so doing we'll open doors into worlds we never knew existed.

Stop for a minute and breathe!

The thing that most people don't do is pause and to stock of their life, and consider what makes them happy and what makes them sad. Sounds simple doesn't it, but we just don't do it. Most of us spend our whole life hiding from our innermost feelings, following the crowd, travelling at breakneck speed and feeling miserable in the process. But, by doing so we fail to pick up important messages that life gives us, and we need these in order to steer our lives in the right direction.

Many people have come to me who have put up with undesirable circumstances for so many years they have forgotten whom they are: people who have been doing the same job for years even though they hate it intensely; people who have endured loveless relationships for far too long; those who have had serious money problems. The list goes on and on. Why do we let this happen?

The sooner we realise that something isn't working in our life the sooner we can do something about it instead of clinging on to it for dear life.

So, I want you to stop right now and take a deep breath. Dig out your journal and complete the following short life quiz.

Exercise

The following list represents eight main areas of your life. I want you to give each area a score between 0 and 10, 10 being perfection and 0 being awful. Take your time, but, most importantly, be honest with yourself.

Your career	0	1	2	3	4	5
6	7	8	9	10		
Money	0	1	2	3	4	5	6
7	8	9	10			
Health	0	1	2	3	4	5
6	7	8	9	10		
Family and friends	0	1	2	3	4
5	6	7	8	9	10	
Partner/romance	0	1	2	3	4
5	6	7	8	9	10	

The Game Of Life

Fun	0	1	2	3	4	5	6
7	8	9	10				

Personal growth		0	1	2	3	4
5	6	7	8	9	10	

Physical environment	0	1	2	3	4
5	6	7	8	9	10

Once you have done this I want you to write down the three areas of your life that scored the lowest.

1 ___Romance___

2 ___Health___

3 ___Growth/Money___

Exercise

Now answer the following questions.

- What is currently making you most unhappy in your life?
- Why have you allowed this to happen?
- What will happen if you continue living in this way?
- How important is it that you make some changes (on a percentage up to 100%)?

- How committed you are to making these changes (on a percentage up to 100%)?

This exercise plays a very important role on your journey to a better life and I will be referring back to your life quiz in the next chapter, so keep it safe.

Don't drain my energy

For most people, as you've just found out, there are a few key areas where it is glaringly obvious that something has gone wrong and change is seriously needed. But, aside from the bigger aspects of our lives, there are also small things that we put up with which are relatively easy to change.

Think about your day-to-day life. If you're constantly looking at unfinished DIY, or if a cascade of clothes falls on your head each time you open your wardrobe doors, it's not going to help you in your quest for a happy life. It's going to drain your energy. I call these small things 'energy drainers' because each time we look at them they make us feel weary. Every time I look at an ever-increasing pile of ironing waiting to be done, or open my 'tax return' folder, my energy levels are drained until I feel depressed and deflated.

What's the cure?

It's time to get rid of them.

Exercise

I want you to think of 20 things, people, circumstances or situations that are sapping your energy, and what do you have to do to eliminate them from your life forever? It might be the broken loo seat, the half-finished decorating, a killer commute to work or selfish friends who talk about themselves constantly.

Make a list of 20 things in your life you that are tolerating – don't worry how small or how big these are – if they are draining your energy write them down.

Now write 20 actions that will eliminate this list forever – from paying your bills by direct debit to employing a cleaner, or having your grocery shopping delivered.

Here's the important part. Lists are wonderful and I'm a huge advocate for them, but they're useless unless you cross things off them. Pin your list where you cannot miss it and make a concerted effort to cross at least one thing off it each week. The satisfaction you'll feel will be well worth it and you will find you have lots more energy in the process!

Philippa's story

Here's a short story about a lady who'd been suppressing her own ambitions and desires for a better life for years, resulting in her feeling very despondent and trapped by her circumstances.

Philippa came to see me a few years ago. She was a beautiful girl in her mid-thirties, very slim with curly blond hair that bounced around her shoulders. She looked a little uncomfortable as I showed her into my office. I offered her a coffee but she declined – I could feel her unease and did my best to make her feel comfortable.

We went through the formalities and moved on to the 'Wheel of Life' exercise (this is similar to the life-quiz exercise above). The 'Wheel of Life' is an exercise in which the client does all the talking and I listen and take notes. It moves clients through each area of their life and they share with me their background and what's currently happening to them. It struck me as we moved around Philippa's wheel that all her scores were relatively high. Now, of course, this never fools me, as everyone has different thresholds. But her life seemed to be in good shape until we got to the 'family and friends' section. I noticed Philippa's body language change as she shuffled from side to side. She sniffed a few times and I could definitely feel her apprehension. She went on to explain that her mother was ill and she was the sole carer for her, even though she had brothers and sisters who lived nearby. I could sense the love Philippa had for her mother, but I could also sense that she was tired and overburdened. We talked at length about her inability to ask for help and how she always found herself saying 'Yes' when she really wanted to say 'No'. Over time this had led people to rely heavily on her and make unreasonable demands on her time. She'd had enough. It was stopping her perusing the things she wanted to do and making her not only exhausted but also downright miserable.

We moved on to set some life-changing goals, which I worked on with Philippa for eight months. As a result I'm pleased to say that she has managed to turn her life around and has created far better balance. Philippa is now retraining as a nurse and should qualify next year.

One thing I notice with all clients is their relief at having shared their problem or concern. We are so used to bottling things up that we rarely share our innermost thoughts with anyone other than ourselves.

By recognising a problem, we are half-way to solving it.

In the next chapter, I'll be showing you how to take your problems areas and turn them into life-changing goals that will leave you bubbling with excitement.

Chapter 2

What do you really want?

Congratulations you've made it to Chapter 2. You've done the tricky bit in deciding what areas of your life need adjusting and have now arrived at one of the most exciting parts of the book.

It's time to be creative and start thinking big. You have now discovered what's not working in your life and it's time to understand what you *really* do want. Sounds simple, doesn't it? Everyone knows what they want, right? Wrong!

Deciding what it is you really want and admitting it, not just to yourself but to others, is probably one of the most frightening and misunderstood undertakings in society today. Just thinking about turning your deep-seated, long-lost dreams into reality is far more frightening for most of us than having root canal treatment at the dentist's – without painkillers!

But, before we delve into the realms of 'Want do I want?' it's important to understand a few things.

At this stage you're probably thinking 'I'm not going to start dreaming now. I'm 40, for God's sake; my life's all right, I've made do and I can't bear any more disappointment.' It's time to let go of this limiting thinking. We all see things we would like to have but don't; we all have places we'd like to visit one day, but haven't; and we all have opportunities we should have taken, but didn't. Sadly we've all been brainwashed into believing that wanting to live a bigger and better life is egoistical and selfish – but it really isn't.

Letting go of a lifetime of programmed denial and disappointment can be terrifying, primarily because it means change. But change is exactly what this book is all about: *positive change*. But, let go we must if we truly want to live a life that makes us happy and feel fulfilled.

It's no wonder we're scared to dream any more. I'm sure we can all remember a time when we were very young, when we told our parents or siblings, 'I want to be a ballet dancer' or 'I want to be a pilot', only to be told to stop fantasising and concentrate on our schoolwork. We found out early in life that the more we wanted something the more we experienced heartache. Even as toddlers who relished exploration we'd hear our mothers cry, 'Don't touch that!' as our tiny little chubby hands reached out for the best vase. Not just once, but time and time again: 'No, no, no, no, no!' By the time we reached our teenage years it was pretty hard to keep our dreams alive beyond what was socially acceptable, of course: passing our driving test or buying our first house. Heaven forbid you should want to own your own company, drive a Ferrari or travel the world! Over time our dreams withered away, leaving us with maybe, just maybe, if we're lucky a few small dreams, or should I say ideas; the ones we knew were achievable. And, I'm afraid to say, it's here we stay, many of us for decades, living our lives in our all too familiar self-created comfort zone.

How depressing!

Dreaming BIG!

Now, when we are deciding what we really want it's important to point out that many people create dreams or goals based upon someone else's demands or opinions. I have clients who come to me saying, 'I want to do my degree because my father says I should.' Or, 'I want to get a second job so I can pay for my daughter's riding lessons.' No! Your dreams should be about what you want, and not what someone else wants you to do. Living your life this way is futile and will in the long run deplete your energy and make you resentful.

This is about you and only you! It's time to be selfish.

OK, so you want a bigger house, a fancy car, four holidays a year and, oh, a new sofa wouldn't go amiss – we all want these things. I want you to be more specific, get beneath the surface and dig deep. Living the life of your dreams has a lot to do with your values, passions and talents, and we'll discuss these in more detail later on.

Of course, your dreams change over the years, and you've probably moved on from wanting the latest *Action Man* figure or a pair of black shiny tap-dancing shoes complete with satin shoelaces. Yet there is still within you an amazing inventory of long-forgotten fantasies. We all have old passions and long-lost dreams that we've put on the back-burner. It's now time to think again and move them to the front of your mind.

What do you *really* want? What are your most deep-seated dreams? Those which you find hard to admit even to yourself let alone others. What are they? What are your most hidden desires, ideas and ambitions, things that you're too scared to dare even whisper out loud? Set your mind free and allow yourself to think big! Really big! I want you to forget that your dreams are too far-fetched or that your friends will think you've gone bonkers or that you're not educated enough. Forget all these things. Just because you've decided to make a dream your reality doesn't mean you having to explain your reasoning to your partner, mum, friends or even yourself. You deserve to live the life you want. Get rid of the notion that you have to be worthy or have to pass some moral test to qualify. It's rubbish. You're worth it! Other people will only water down your dreams, just as they always have done. We arrived on this earth to play, to create and, ultimately, to experience joy in the process. You have one decision to make – just one – and that is to be happy. What is it that will make you smile from the inside out?

Now the challenge is to peel the onion through layers of 'should', 'shouldn't' and 'No', and see what lies beneath. One analogy may be: 'It's like holding a huge catalogue in your hand, and within it is every career, experience or dream you could possibly imagine having. Your job is to place your order.' How amazing would that be! Well, it's time to start browsing.

Making the dream real

I want you now to look back at the life quiz you completed in Chapter 1 and reconnect with the three main areas of your life in which you scored the least.

What we're about to attempt is the most important thing you'll ever do. You're about to create three life-changing goals that will transform your existence for the better. I want you to take your three lowest-scoring life areas and set one life-changing goal in each, unless you already have a specific goal in mind. But, before you eagerly race off to do this there are five things you need to keep in mind as you lay down your goals. These are:

- Your goal must be your goal, not someone else's.
- Your goal must be specific. Don't be too vague!
- Your goal must be positive and inspire and motivate you.
- Your goal must be achievable within a 12-month time span.
- Your goal must be measurable in some way.

It's very important how you frame your goal and the type of language you use. Let me explain. All three of your goals should excite you. Now, I know from experience that when we set goals, although they may well excite us they also can scare the hell out of us at the same time, and this is perfectly normal. Most people who experience a whiff of fear just curl up into a ball until the fear subsides. What they fail to realise is that fear is just a normal part of life, which comes into play when we extend the boundaries of our comfort zones. We must embrace fear and not run away from it. Every successful person has felt fear at some point, they may not call it 'fear', but I promise you they definitely experienced some discomfort on their journey to success. Period!

Remember, a good goal should both excite and scare you at the same time. The idea is that your goals should feel uncomfortable, because if they don't then they are probably too easy! We'll discuss how to tackle fear in far greater depth in the final chapter.

What you also want to avoid is setting goals that use negative terminology. For example, let's say you want to lose two stone in weight; you might decide that your goal is 'Finally, to be thin'. Think about this for a second, what does this goal imply? It implies that, first, by wanting to be thin you are currently not, and, second, by using the word 'finally', you are subconsciously saying that you've tried many times before to be thin, and have failed. Can you see what I'm getting at? Every time you read this goal to yourself you're likely to feel discouraged and apathetic rather than excited! Not a good start. A better goal might be: 'To buy a pair of size 12 jeans'. Now that conjurers up much better mental images than the first one. It creates a vision of being slim, slender and happy with your body image.

Let me give you some examples of both good and bad goal-setting.

Example 1

- To start my new photography business by January (Good goal).

- To get out of my current job and become a photographer (Bad goal).

Example 2

- To meet Mr Right by the end of the year (Good goal).

- Not to feel lonely any more (Bad goal).

Example 3

- To find my purpose in life (Good goal).

- To stop feeling so bored and unfulfilled (Bad goal).

Another important aspect to goal-setting is not to be too vague. Your goals must be specific; if not, how will you know if you've achieved them? Putting a deadline such as 'by January' or 'by the spring' really gives your goal some depth and accountability. Now, I understand that some goals are long-term ones, and may take a few years, but if a goal is set too far in the future it's extremely hard to keep motivated and on track. If it is a long-term goal just break it down into small chunks and make sure that whatever target you set is achievable within a 12-month time-span.

Lastly, measurability is extremely important as it gives you a start and a finish point. Without some way of measuring your goals, or your successes, how on earth will you know if you've achieved them? For example, weight, money, happiness, confidence. Make sure you have some way of gauging your accomplishments!

OK, I think we are all set to take the first step towards your new life. Here's the question: What are your three goals going to be?

What most people tend to find when setting their three goals is that they have one or two bigger goals and one smaller goal. That's perfectly normal.

If you're still finding it difficult to decide what your goals should be, the following exercise should help to inspire you.

Exercise

- Did you ever have a childhood dream; if so, what was it?
- Is there anything you're naturally good at, or that you find comes easily to you?
- What do you love to do in your spare time?
- Is there anything you're passionate about in life?
- If you had no limitations, such as lack of money or education, what would you love to do?
- What long-lost dreams have you been putting on the back-burner for the past 5, 10 or 15 years?

- What is currently missing from your life?
- Is there anything you've seen or heard on the TV, in a magazine or maybe from a friend or colleague which sparked some interest for you recently; if so, what was it?
- What's the one thing you want to do before you die?
- What goals might you set which could make the biggest difference to your life?

Having worked with many people who have set all sorts of life-changing goals, from business-related to personal or spiritual goals, I have compiled a list of genuine goals, which my clients have set, just to get your juices flowing.

- 'To set up my lama-trekking farm by next April'
- 'To launch my coffee shop and have a champagne party to celebrate'
- 'To pass my bike test and organise a charity run before my fortieth birthday'
- 'To move to Australia within 12 months'
- 'To retrain and work abroad in an animal rescue centre'
- 'To turn £10 into £6000 by this time next year'
- 'To design and build my own house'
- 'To reach spiritual enlightenment'
- 'To release my debut album'

- 'To get to know "me" better'
- 'To climb to the top of Mount Kilimanjaro and raise £10,000 for charity'
- 'To reach my target weight'
- 'To wake up every morning with a smile on my face'
- 'To pay £20,000 from my mortgage within one year and become financially FREE'
- 'To have a turnover in excess of £150,000 by June'
- 'To complete my first book and get it published before my baby is born'
- 'To take up tennis again and start competing by the end of the year'
- 'To go to Africa and work as a volunteer for Save The Children'.

This is it – time to create your life-changing goals.

Exercise

This is it! Write your three goals down in your journal.

Goal 1:_____

_____

Goal 2:_____

_____

Goal 3:_____

_____

Still stuck?

If you're still having trouble defining your goal, or goals, stop. Put down this book, shut your journal and do something else. There is no rush. Go for a walk, play with the kids, have a cuppa, do the ironing. Take your mind off it for a while. No one is demanding that you decide here and now, so don't put pressure on yourself. Take a break and come back to it later. What you'll find is that when you're cooking dinner or are in the shower, an idea will pop into your head. When it does, the dinner can wait. Go and write it your journal! You can't force inspiration; like a baby, it arrives when it's ready.

Once you have listed your three life-enhancing goals I want you to complete the following exercise by asking yourself four very important questions.

Exercise

- Is this really my goal?
- Am I committed to achieving this goal?
- Does this goal excite me?
- Will achieving this goal make me feel happy?

What you're looking for here is a resounding 'Yes' in answer to all four questions. If you don't hear it, ask yourself why? If you have decided on a particular goal because your partner thinks it's a good idea it will not work. If you have set a goal you're not committed to it will not work. If you've set a goal that doesn't inspire or motivate you it will not work. And, finally, if achieving your goal won't make you happy, what's the point?

You know, deep down, when you've set the right goals because they feel right. If you're pondering too much then you haven't set the right goal, so move on to something else.

How do you know if you've set the right goals?

- You feel extremely excited and scared at the same time.
- You feel like jumping up and down on the spot.
- You feel impatient and immediately start researching

your goals.

- You wake up in the morning and for the first time in years you have a smile on your face.
- You phone your mum, sister, brother or friends to share your overwhelming excitement.

Now I want you to do something extremely important. I want you to go and get a blank piece of paper and write down your three goals clearly and concisely. Do them in different colours: colour them in, make them stand out. Once you have done this go and pin your goals sheet where you will see it every single day: on the bathroom mirror, the fridge door or on your computer screen. It really doesn't matter, but I want you to ensure that you will see your goals every day, so think carefully.

Peering into the black hole

I'm now going to do something rather odd. I'm going to take you into your own personal black hole (only for a few minutes you'll be pleased to hear). I'm not one for negativity as it's a huge energy-drainer, but there's a rationale behind this next exercise, honestly!

I want you to imagine what your life will be like if you don't come out of denial and make some positive changes. Imagine 12 months has passed, you've totally forgotten about this little book and it's now tucked away on a shelf somewhere gathering dust, and nothing in your life has really changed. You're in the same position you are in today. You're still driving the same journey to work, you're still sitting at the same desk, looking at the same computer screen, you're still broke by the tenth of the month and, deplorably, you're still feeling unhappy and dissatisfied. You get the picture? Nothing has moved forwards. How will you be feeling? Stagnant, depressed, miserable, disheartened, frustrated, angry, unfulfilled, disgruntled, and stuck in the same old rut.

Ask yourself: 'What will happen if I do nothing to change my life?'

Not a pretty thought. Hey! Let's stop here. Enough is enough. I'm just trying to get you to see that life without change is the same as deciding that everything will remain the same.

So, are you ready to make some changes to your life and make this the year that catapults you forwards into a brand new reality?

There is a reason why you're reading this book. Somewhere deep inside you, you want change. You want a better life, and you hear the ever so quiet whispers inside that are nudging you forwards. The time is now; the time has come for you to take control and start really living! Are you ready to experience what your life will be like when you've achieved your goals?

Seeing your new life in full colour

In order to help keep you focused and excited about your goals, I want you to create a future vision of your life once you have actually achieved them. Visualisation is used by some very successful people, from authors to businessmen, from entrepreneurs to Olympic athletes. Almost every athlete plays their event through in the mind before the start. They feel the muscles they will use, how each one will tense and how much power is behind a jump or a sprint. Every successful person will tell you the same thing: they could see their success long before it happened. I remember deciding that I didn't want to work in advertising and marketing any longer. I was fed up with sitting in the same office, with the same people, doing the same work year in and year out, whilst my daughter was at nursery being cared for by someone else. I wanted more freedom, more fulfilment, and I wanted to stop wishing my life away from one weekend to the next. I had no idea what I wanted to do at the time. All I knew was that I wanted to do something worthwhile, something that made a difference to the world and something that would fit around motherhood whilst earning me the money I needed to sustain my standard of living.

I remember that each night, before I went to sleep, I would spend a few minutes imagining how I wanted my life to be. I would envisage it was five years into the future and note all the changes that had taken place during that time. I could see myself with two small children. I could see my vegetable garden lush with marrows, carrots, potatoes and the like. I could see how wonderful my home looked with all the improvements we'd made. I could see as a family we were financially secure and I could see myself running a business from home that fitted perfectly around my family life, giving me the freedom I desired. Every time I visualised and imagined how I wanted my life to be, I'd feel an overwhelming sense of peace and happiness, and I'd drift off to sleep with ease. I still do this exercise even to this day, and I always will, because it feels so good! Little did I know when I started doing this that very slowly but surely, one by one, these things I'd imagined would start to manifest in my life. I did start to grow my own organic vegetables. We did make vast improvements to our home. Our savings did expand nicely and I did create my own business, working from home as a life coach and writer. I had created exactly what I had imagined in my mind's eye.

Just 15 minutes of creative visualisation a day can change your life in unimaginable ways. It's just that most people don't believe in the power of their own imagination. Do not underestimate this magical power. There has been extensive research into visualisation and the power of intention, and we'll be delving into this in more depth later on.

Enough about me and my vision, it's time to start creating yours!

If you're a non-visual person or have difficultly holding images in your mind, simply write your vision down on a piece of paper or even create a 'vision board' full of pictures cut from magazines, which represent how you want your future to look.

OK, ready?

Exercise

Make sure you are comfortable and won't be disturbed for at least the next five minutes. Take 30 seconds or so to relax and breathe in and out deeply. When you feel ready, close your eyes and begin visualising your future reality as if it's already manifested. If you're non-visual, write down the answers to the questions below instead. Imagine you have moved into the future and have now achieved all your goals and dreams.

- When you first open your eyes in the morning and the first glimpse of sunlight is gleaming in through your window, what do you see?
- When we get out of bed and look out the window, what is the weather like today?
- Who do you share your life with and how you feel about them?
- How do you behave around each other?
- What are you wearing today/how do you look, and how do you feel about yourself?
- How do you spend your morning?
- How do you spend your afternoon?
- How do you spend your evenings, and with whom?
- How are you feeling about your life?

Look back over the last 12 months and marvel at all the wonderful things you have achieved, feel the feelings of success, satisfaction and fulfilment at just how perfect your life is now you've achieve your dreams. Daydream for as long you feel comfortable and, when you're ready, bring your awareness back to the present, wiggle your toes, take a deep breath and smile.

You've just taken the first step towards making your goals a reality! Not only are you, on one level, helping to attract your goals, but on a very basic level visualising keeps your dreams alive: it keeps the passion and enthusiasm burning inside you, and that's what you need if you want to turn your life around.

I'd like you to commit to spending five minutes doing this exercise every day, maybe in the shower when getting ready for work or maybe in the evening just before you go to bed.

Alison's story

Here is a story about a lady who had been putting her life-long dream on the back-burner for years, until one day she decided she'd done enough procrastinating and was going to do something about it.

Alison was in her early forties and had two teenage sons. She'd spent most of her working life in a bank and, moving from post to post, had progressed within the organization. She neither hated nor enjoyed her job. It was easy and she'd done it for so long that she couldn't imagine doing anything else. She was 'part of the furniture', as she put it. I distinctly remember picking up on her bubbly personality and enthusiasm.

The goals we set were relatively straightforward. The first concerned having more '*me* time' so Alison could spend quality time nurturing herself (something that had stopped happening as a result of being a mother and working full-time). The second was about meeting new people locally and expanding her friendships; the third goal was to get fit and healthy. Even though we laid down Alison's goals with relative ease (she'd obviously given it some thought before she attended the session), I felt she was holding back somewhat. There was something she wasn't sharing. I asked a few probing questions and it didn't take long before Alison admitted that she had a long-lost childhood dream but had never had the courage to pursue it. She kept saying that I would think it was daft and would laugh. As if I would!

Alison told me that she'd always been a keen animal-lover, starting when she was very young. She explained how she used to dress up her tabby cat in doll's clothes and push him around the garden in her doll's pushchair (poor cat, I didn't ask how long he'd lived!). She went on to explain that her main love was dogs. Any dogs, big, small, fat thin. She just loved all dogs, and I could tell by the way her eyes sparkled when we talked about them that they were obviously very close to her heart. Alison loved dogs so much she even did 'dog sitting' for friends and neighbours while they are away on holiday. The problem was her husband, who was allergic to animals, and, you've guessed it, dogs as well so they could never have any animal at home. Short of getting rid of her husband the only real option open to Alison was to look after everyone else's animals whenever she could.

It turned out that her dream was to set up a dog training school. Alison had attended classes with her own dogs many years ago when she still lived at home, and she often used to help the trainer at the local dog training school from time to time. After she'd told me this Alison sat back in her chair and smiled with the sense of relief at having told me her dream and looked at me, waiting for my response.

Alison's third goal became: 'To open my first dog training academy within 12 months'. I was delighted for her, and she was ecstatic that, for the first time in her life, someone had taken her dream seriously and was going to help her achieve it. Needless to say she left the session flying high!

It took Alison 14 months to retrain, find premises, set up her business and leave her job at the bank. Now she runs a successful dog training school and is living her dream. All it took was one decision!

Chapter 3

What's going on in your head?

So now you have created three exciting goals and displayed them somewhere you'll see them every day. What next? Before we start getting into physical action we still have some work to do, and by this I mean 'inner work'. I want you to put your goals to one side for a moment. I'm not talking about forgetting them; on the contrary, I'll be showing you later on the secret of how to make your dreams into reality. But, before we breathe life into your goals we have some very important topics to cover which will help you not only achieve your goals but also manifest a wonderful existence for the rest of your life. I want to talk to you about your programming. Changing your life for the better starts by changing what you believe is possible.

Here's what is probably running through your mind right now: 'I think my goals are great in theory, but I can't see how on earth this book is going to help me to achieve them, it's impossible' or 'It's nice to dream, but it isn't going to happen' or 'I haven't got time to do this'.

Sounds familiar?

I've been there. I understand. But I promise it's only a change in perception that is needed in order for you to achieve your goals. Nothing more!

Your faulty programming

We come into this world with a wonderful individual, unique blueprint that holds within it our personality, talents, passions and values. It is these things which make us who we are. There are people who have natural talents for making people laugh, for healing or for nature. There are people who have natural talents for creating inspiring works of art, for playing a musical instrument or who have the ability to sing in tune effortlessly. It's these differences which make our world such a diverse place in which to live. Thank goodness! We wouldn't all want to fancy the same person or pursue the same dreams in life.

Although we have our unique personality and talents, there is a part of our brain that is untouched and open to programming with whatever we choose. From very early on in life we are consistently creating new habits, beliefs and behaviours which become 'hard-wired' into our subconscious mind. In fact, it has been said that almost all our beliefs, habits and behaviours are created before the age of seven. Yes, really! I like to think of the brain as a jelly: – every impression made by our parents, siblings, teachers, nation, religion and culture leaves its mark in some way. And sometimes these impressions may mask our unique blueprint.

For example, when a toddler first learns to walk, he or she takes some time to master the skill and get balancing just right. Each time the child falls and gets back up to try again he or she is creating a new neuro-pathway in the brain. Eventually, when the child finally conquers the art of putting one foot in front of the other, the neuro-pathway is hard-wired into the brain and walking becomes a habit and is therefore effortless. The child can walk without having to think about it. Remember when you were earning to drive a car, or learning to read: these skills all eventually become habitual.

Our understanding of ourselves and the world around us is created and hard-wired in exactly the same way. So, what are beliefs? A set of (perhaps rash) generalisations made – about others, about life in general and about ourself. They form our version of reality, based on what we feel and perceive about our experiences.

What you think and believe will affect the way you behave and perform, and influence the actions you take; and will shape your life as you know it.

So let's go back to the concept of the jelly. Our parents' beliefs are generally passed down to us. Our parents pass on these beliefs in order to protect us (so they think). Maybe you were discouraged from pursuing a particular talent because your parents thought you ought to be doing something more practical. Or perhaps as a young child you observed your siblings getting more positive attention than you did and therefore formed the belief that somehow you weren't good enough. Or maybe your parents constantly told you how unsafe the outside world was and you formed a belief that we live in a dangerous world.

All these kinds of beliefs are destructive interpretations of ourselves and the world around us; and they lie within our subconscious mind and we're not even aware that they exist.

Now, here's the really fascinating part.

The beliefs we create are not based on fact. They are simply opinions. There is never any hard evidence to support them. But, amazingly, we build our lives around these beliefs every day because we think they are facts. They become the foundation for what we experience in our adult life. If, as a child, you were constantly told that money was tight, you'll keep a tight hold on your money as an adult. If you were told never to trust anyone you'll spend your whole life watching your back and being suspicious of people. If you were told you weren't clever enough at school you'll live your adult life thinking you're not good enough. Can you see what I'm getting at?

And the truly startling part: *once we have formed a belief we will continue to live our life by it.*

We continue to find evidence to support this way of thinking. Think about it for a second. Your brain is consistently showing you evidence to support your belief, even though it's not a fact! And your brain will instantly dismiss anything that contradicts that belief. Perhaps someone genuinely pays you a lovely compliment and you dismiss it by saying, 'Oh, it was nothing. Anyway, it wasn't really my doing.' Your underlying belief is telling you not to accept the compliment because it doesn't fit with your belief and therefore must be untrue.

If you were told as a child that you were ugly or fat, or that your brother or sister was more attractive than you, you quickly form a belief that 'I'm fat' or 'I'm ugly', and that belief is hard-wired into the brain. The brain's job is then to reinforce that belief by showing you evidence to support it in your day-to-day life. It might be that every time you look in the mirror your focus goes directly to your nose, your flat chest or your big bum. You will pick out what you consider to be your faults and dismiss any of the good bits. Now, remember, thinking that you are fat or ugly is just a belief, it's not fact! It is something you were told, that you decided was true and was therefore worth believing. The problem is that you take this belief into your adult life and it affects everything you do. It affects your confidence and your self-esteem. It affects the people you mix with and where you go. In short, it affects your whole life! Now can you see how destructive a limiting belief may be?

It's the same with money, love, education, health, career, family and so on. You need to become aware of what you believe about yourself and your world.

We all become very good at finding evidence to support our beliefs, and we do this subconsciously – without question. Why? And how does this happen? It is because of what biological psychology calls the 'reticular activating system' (RAS).

The RAS is a cluster of brain cells which acts like a radar system activated by our beliefs. The RAS filters in information that is consistent with what we believe, and filters out anything that does not support our thoughts. Our findings are backed up by self-talk such as 'I knew that was going to happen', 'That's just my luck' and 'I'm not good enough to do that.'

Together, our RAS and our self-talk form a comfort zone which represents the limits of our ability, based on our beliefs.

A simple exercise to demonstrate this theory: try to spot how many people are walking down the street wearing a red top. Having spent time counting people who are wearing red tops, try and remember how many other people were wearing green tops. The chances are you won't remember how many green tops you saw. You know there were some, but your attention was drawn to spotting red tops only.

You can see just how powerful the mind really is. You must remember that your brain is a wonderful tool, and *you* have the power to 'program' it whichever way you want. Most of the beliefs you hold within you serve you well and will continue to serve you well for the rest of your days. The problem arises when you allow past limiting beliefs to guide your present and future decisions. These negative beliefs will stop you achieving your true potential, and I believe that limiting beliefs are the biggest barrier to us achieving success in our lives. Limiting beliefs keep us trapped in our comfort zone; they keep us on the treadmill. In order for you to achieve your goals you're going to need to become aware of any self-limiting beliefs that could potentially get in the way and sabotage your success.

Let's blame the parents!

You are not responsible for the way you were raised, but you are responsible for what you do now. The past is past, you can't change it so don't get hung up on trying to pin the blame on your parents or anyone else for that matter. Ignorance is bliss. Your parents can't teach you something they were not aware of themselves. Instead, try visualising them as small, young, defenceless children themselves. See them with their little chubby faces, looking all innocent and helpless; now, think about where they grew up, the type of childhood they had, their parents. Where do you think their limiting beliefs came from?

Please don't blame anyone for the beliefs you hold. They are no one's fault, and channelling your energy into blaming others won't serve you well. It will just make you bitter and that certainly won't help you move forwards on your path of self-discovery.

This book is about *you taking control of your life now*. Here – and now – is where your power lies.

Some common limiting beliefs

I have listed some of the most common limiting beliefs I have encountered in my life-coaching practice. As you read the list ask yourself if you believe any of them (or a variation on them) and, if you do, ask yourself why you believe them.

- 'I'm not clever enough'
- 'I'm not educated enough'
- 'I have no special talent'
- 'I'm not attractive enough'
- 'I'm not strong enough'
- 'I'm not gifted'
- 'It always works for everyone else, but not for me'
- 'There's a finite amount of money I can earn'
- 'Bad things always happen to me'
- 'I never win anything'
- 'Nobody likes me'
- 'Rich people are untrustworthy and selfish'
- 'Life's hard'
- 'I can't trust anyone'
- 'This world is a dangerous place'
- 'I am always getting ill'
- 'I have a slow metabolism and that's why I'm overweight'.

I'm not one for delving into the past to find out why we have limiting beliefs, or from whom they came. Yes, it's very important to uncover a limiting belief and find out where it originated, but nothing more. All we need to know is *what our limiting beliefs are*: from there we have the power to do something about them. As I've said before, no one is to blame for them and going back into the past really doesn't serve you well. It may be more destructive than the limiting belief itself.

Here's the good news: *you can change a limiting belief.*

Hooray, that's a relief isn't it! Let me explain. Just because a neuro-pathway has been created and hard-wired doesn't mean it can't be 'rewired'. Think of your brain as a mass of circuits and connections, and just like rewiring your house, you can rewire your brain.

Here's a good example. When someone has a stroke, normally the lack of oxygen to the brain means that in certain areas the neuro-pathways die away. It tends to affect the speech or the ability to walk, read or write, and so on. So, arguably, stroke patients almost regress to being children in some ways. They then have to start the process of having to learn to talk, walk, read or write again. And the amazing thing is that they do! Of course it takes time, but they start forming new connections in the brain and eventually master the skills once more. My point here is that you have the ability to change a belief, a habit or even a behavioural pattern, even if you've been running it for the last 20, 30 or even 50 years of your life.

Remember, your brain is like an incredible bio-computer; all you need to do is install the software and watch the magic unfold.

But before we get to the exciting bit about how to change a belief, I want to talk to you about your habits and 'behavioural masks'.

What are your behavioural masks?

'What's a behavioural mask?' I hear you say. Well, the only way I can describe a behavioural mask is as an overcoat that we decide to put on when we interact with the world around us. When a particularly strong negative belief takes hold of us we create a behavioural mask that we put on subconsciously. It's like a protective barrier which covers up our true self.

For example, if, when you were a child, you lived in a large family and the only time you ever got any attention was when you had a problem or were hurt, you probably formed the belief that 'to be loved I must have a problem'. It was a good way to get attention and when you got that attention you received the love you so needed and craved. So, how does this translate into your adult life? In order to get attention as a child you created a behavioural mask to get your needs met, and even though 30 years have now passed, you are still acting out that same behaviour pattern. Have you ever met a hypochondriac or someone who always seems to have one problem after another? Have you ever wondered why they act in this way? Although this type of behaviour may be very effective as a child by the time we reach adulthood, it is outdated and can cause us lots of problems. Nobody really wants to spend time with someone who always seems to be ill or who has lots of problems. In fact, acting this way will have the opposite effect. To start with people will want to help you, and they will do everything they can, but eventually they will get fed up with you whining and whinging, and will leave you, which – of course – just backs up the original belief. It's a vicious circle.

I'm not saying that everyone who holds this type of belief will act in this way, it's just an example. But what I am saying is that, as a human being, we do tend to create some odd habits and behaviours in order to compensate for our unmet needs and limiting beliefs.

Once you can identify that you are wearing a behavioural mask, or even a few different masks, you can decide whether they are serving you well or not. Although it can be a very liberating experience, it may be extremely uncomfortable to discover a particular behavioural mask you've been using for many years. It can feel like someone has stolen all your clothes and you're running around naked trying to find them. But, don't worry, this book is about self-discovery, and that means peeling off all the layers, one by one, that you've acquired over the years and discovering who you really are! Behaviour is just another layer. One important thing to remember is that beneath each of the masks listed below lies a limiting belief of some description. See if you can work out what the belief might be for each one.

Are you ready to have a look at some typical masks?

- The *poser*: this is the type of person who likes to be centre of attention all the time. You're only truly happy when everyone is looking at you. You hate being on your own and are generally quite loud and flamboyant.

- The *super hero:* these people are always running around helping people and playing the 'hero'. They get more joy out of helping others than they do by helping themselves. They're always busy doing something for someone else; they never get time for themselves. In fact, they just seem to attract people into their life who need help.

- The *bullshitter*: they are always telling wild stories about their amazing lives. They like to boast about their so-called accomplishments and often find themselves lying in order to look good, and end up in all sorts of tricky predicaments. They have no real substance, and people never know when they're being honest.

- The *comedian*: this person is always joking around and playing daft tricks on people. They're always the ones who crack the first joke, they struggle to be serious for long and find it difficult to be around solemn people.

- The *dizzy blond*: we all know the person who always says daft things and comes across as generally unworldly, almost a bit dim. They are often referred to as 'a bit blond'. They're always looking for someone to rescue you and take responsibility for them.

- The *bully*: this is the type of person who comes across as very intimidating. They like to be heard, and don't like anyone who opposes their decisions. They're generally very loud and belligerent, and they like to be the centre of attention.

- The *pessimist*: these people believe 'it's too good to be true' or 'it'll never last'. They never trust anyone and are always cynical. Their glass is always half-empty and they always find the negative in any situation.

- The *anarchist*: they like to be different and go against the grain. They hate any type of authority – like the boss, tax inspector, traffic warden or police.

- The *injured party*: this is the type of person who is always in some kind of crisis. Something bad is always happening to them, whether they are being sacked, breaking up with their partner yet again, bumping their car or simply having a bad day.

- The *speed demon*: these people never sit down for any longer than five minutes. They are always rushing around, generally because they have left everything to the last minute.

- The *obsessive*: this is the type of person who likes to do everything themselves because only they know best. They are perfectionists; it's not right unless it's done exactly the way they like it.

- The *sex god/temptress*: he or she is a terrible flirt. They like to know that people around them are attracted to them. They enjoy seducing people and once they know they've got someone in the palm of their hand, they lose interest.

- *The cameleon*: this is the type of person who changes their personality or voice to suit the situation they're in. If they're talking to someone who is well-off, they mention that fact they drive a Mercedes; if they're talking to someone less affluent they adapt their story, telling him or her how much in debt they are. They are constantly changing their life story in order to fit in.

There you have it. Behavioural masks revealed! So, which one (or ones) fit you?

Exercise
Write down your top three behavioural masks and the underlying belief you think you're compensating for? (For example, I always play the 'temptress' because it feeds me with the love I'm craving for and makes me feel esteemed and appreciated).

Mask 1 _____

_____

Limiting belief causing mask is_____

_____

Mask 2 _____

_____

Limiting belief causing mask is_____

_____

Mask 3 _____

_____

Limiting belief causing mask is_____

_____

Yes, it can be quite hard to come to terms with the fact
that you've been hiding behind a particular behavioural

mask for most of your life. But it may be therapeutic and healing at the same time. If you want to find out who you really are, you need to know what subconscious behaviours you are creating in your daily life.

When I first uncovered my behavioural masks (and, yes, there was more than one) I felt like someone had stripped me of my personality. Remember, though, it's not your *real* personality you're letting go of but a behaviour you've create as a result of a limiting belief you hold. Letting go of a particular behaviour lets the 'real' you come to the surface.

The real you is someone who isn't trying to be someone they're not; you're not performing or bending yourself into some bizarre outward appearance in order to try and impress people, or fit in with the crowd. You will be yourself, saying what you really think without having to even think about it. Can you imagine how nice it would be to be your true self? To be less false, less tense and completely comfortable with yourself – probably for the first time in your life.

One point I'd like to make here is that when we start to change a behavioural pattern that we've been running for a long time those around us will be a bit concerned or confused: 'Why aren't you flirting with me anymore?', 'Why have you stopped cracking so many jokes?', 'Why aren't you joining in with the Monday morning gossip?' But don't let this deter you: you can't be something you're not just to please someone else. Remember, this is your journey.

Now, it's all very well uncovering your behavioural masks, but you can't really drop them until you address what the limiting belief behind each mask actually is, and that's what we're going to be doing next. Once you can change a limiting belief for a healthier one your behaviour will change automatically.

Let's rewire the house!

Now we've looked at your limiting beliefs and behavioural patterns the next step is to decide to change a particular belief or behaviour that is limiting you in some way. Start with one belief at a time and then move on to others later on. It's a bit like going to the gym in January. You're raring to go; you can see the benefits of getting fit and are desperate to start seeing results immediately. If you are anything like me you start off by going five times a week, but by the second week you've dropped down to four times, by the third week you're going twice and by the end of January you've stopped going altogether. When introducing a new habit or routine into your life don't make it too hard for yourself or you'll run out of stream far too quickly and give up! Be kind to yourself, there's no rush. It has taken you all your life to get where you are now, so don't expect things to change overnight.

Try this: fold your arms in front of you, the way you would normally fold them. Come on, fold your arms; it'll only take a second! Are they folded? Now notice how familiar and comfortable it feels. Now, unfold your arms and fold them the opposite way. Can you feel how unnatural and strange it feels? If I were to tell you that from now on you could only fold your arms in this 'new' way it would take a certain amount of time and effort before it became habitual. It's simply because your brain likes to follow the same pattern and when you try to change or introduce something new it protests. You need a degree of commitment and time when deciding to change a limiting belief or behaviour pattern. Without your commitment, nothing will change. We seem to think that just because we've uncovered a limiting belief or a less than desirable behavioural pattern, somehow that is enough. It's not! You need to take some physical action in order to change any aspect of your life.

Exercise

Make it your intention to start noticing the beliefs of those around you. Notice the things people say in their general conversation. If you listen carefully you'll be able to hear their personal beliefs seeping through. Observe your partner, your children, your hairdresser, your friends, your boss, the check-out lady in Tesco. Study the language of pessimistic people and that of those of a sunnier disposition. It's very interesting! The reason I'm asking you to do this is because it's far easier to notice the language, habits and behaviors of others than it is to observe our own.

Do this exercise for at least one week. You'll be amazed at what you discover.

Exercise

I want you to get your own beliefs clear now. Everyone has hundreds of different beliefs, some good and some bad, but no doubt you'll have a few fundamental ones that have really shaped your life as you know it. Take 20 minutes to do a 'mind dump' on a large blank piece of paper, and list all your beliefs about every aspect of your life – both big and small. I want you to think of the beliefs you hold in the areas of your life listed below. Write as many good and bad beliefs as you can think of, concerning:

- relationships
- work or career
- personal image
- personality
- health
- finances
- the way you see the world.

Now use your 'mind dump' to devise two separate lists, one of all the negative beliefs and one of all the positive beliefs you hold. Once you have done this look at your negative list and underline the three beliefs that are having the most impact on your life ('I never have enough money', 'I'm unattractive', 'I'll never find a job I'm happy in', for example).

List your top three limiting beliefs below.

Limiting belief 1_____

Limiting belief 2_____

Limiting belief 3_____

Exercise

Now answer the following questions for each of your three negative beliefs. It's important that you understand the impact your negative beliefs are having on your life.

- In what way is this belief unfounded?
- Where did this belief come from (your mother, your teacher, your best friend)?
- How has this belief limited you in your life so far?
- What does holding this belief cost you on a daily, weekly or monthly basis?
- What will happen if you continue to hold this belief?

Can you see what impact your limiting belief is having on your life? Remember, each and every day you are living your life by the rules of the beliefs you hold – isn't it about time you dropped the ones that hold you back?

Once you have revealed the top three limiting beliefs you'd like to work on, and looked at the impact they are currently having, ask yourself, 'Am I ready and committed to changing these beliefs?' If you're not, ask yourself, 'How are these beliefs and behaviours serving me in some way?' When you feel committed and ready to move on the next step in the process is consciously to choose to create new healthier beliefs to replace the old ones: beliefs that will help you to expand, to grow and, ultimately, move out of your comfort zone to live a bigger and better life.

Creating a new belief is extremely simple. It's really a case of stating the opposite to your limiting belief, as in the list below.

- 'I'm not clever enough' will become '*I am clever enough*'.
- 'I'm not gifted/educated enough' becomes '*I am educated*'.
- 'I have no special talent' becomes '*I have many hidden talents*'.
- 'I'm not attractive enough' becomes '*I am attractive in many ways*'.
- 'I'm not strong enough' becomes '*I am physically and emotionally strong*'.
- 'It always works for everyone else but not for me' becomes '*There is no reason it can't work for me*'.
- 'There's a finite amount of money I can earn' becomes '*There is money for everyone in the world*'.
- 'Bad things always happen to me' will become '*Good things happen to me all the time*'.
- 'I never win anything' becomes '*I am open to winning things*'.
- 'Nobody like me' becomes '*There are a lot of people*

who enjoy my company'.

- 'Rich people are untrustworthy and selfish' becomes '*Rich people are the same as everyone else*'.
- 'Life's hard' becomes '*Life's easy and a joy*'.
- 'I can't trust anyone' becomes '*There are a lot of people in my life whom I can trust*'.
- 'This world is a dangerous place' becomes '*This world is a safe place for me to live in*'.
- 'I am always getting ill' becomes '*Every day I feel healthier and healthier*'.
- 'I have a slow metabolism and that's why I'm overweight' becomes '*I no longer retain weight*'.

Exercise

Looking at the three limiting beliefs you listed above, work out what your top three new beliefs need to be ('Money is now flowing freely into my life', 'I am attractive', 'I am working in my perfect job', for example).

New belief 1 _____

New belief 2 _____

New belief 3 _____

_____

How will adapting to each of these new beliefs change your life?

New belief 1 will _____

_____

New belief 2 will _____

_____

New belief 3 will _____

_____

Now, I know you're probably sitting there thinking, 'Well, this is all very nice, but I don't believe these new beliefs.' Hang fire! Rome wasn't built in a day, so stop being impatient!

When you first create a new belief it may not seem true, and I know this because I've been there, but think of your new belief as a small seed. You and I both know that seeds don't just develop and bloom overnight, even with help from Miracle-Gro® plant food! What we're talking about here is creating a brand-new neuro-pathway in the brain, and doing this will take time. Remember the earlier armfolding exercise? And, if you're wondering how long it will take, unfortunately I can't tell you: it all depends on you and how committed you are.

Below I have outlined three ways to re-program your subconscious mind with a new belief. There are lots of different ways of doing this, but I have come up with what I have found to be the three most successful methods, and these are as follows.

- Creating evidence.
- Affirmations.
- Visualisation.

Let's take each one and break it down.

Creating evidence

Like its name suggests, this method entails writing a list of evidence to support your new belief. What I mean by this is creating a list of things, situations, events and conversations which back up or prove that your new belief is true. This will help to form a new pathway in the brain. For example, if your old limiting belief is 'I'm unattractive' and you have decided that your new belief is 'I am attractive' your list of evidence would include things like compliments you have received from people, or times in your life when you felt at your best, maybe your wedding day or twenty-first birthday. You're simply listing evidence that will support your new belief. So sit down and give yourself an hour or so to really think about it. Go somewhere quiet, where you can escape the normal pressures of life. You might find it difficult to think of things at first, but keep going; once you get into the swing of it you'll find the evidence will start to flow. If you find it really hard then keep coming back to your list over a couple of days. One of my clients went through her diary at the end of each week and wrote down all her accomplishments – from walking the dog, mowing the lawn and meeting someone new to winning new business. What a great idea!

Now this is the most important part of this exercise – once you have created your list you must make an effort to refer to it every day. We're only talking about a few minutes a day, nothing too strenuous. Not only will this help you to see that your old beliefs are simply unfounded, but it'll help you to remember more evidence and, more importantly, reading the list every day will help you to start creating that new, much-needed pathway in your brain. But you must make a commitment to read it as much as possible. For me, I put my list in my *filoFax* because I know I will have to open it every day and my evidence will fall out, which in turn prompts me to read it. Perhaps a bedside table or the fridge door is best for you, anywhere you cannot miss it. You might even put it in a shoe – it all depends on how serious you are!

Affirmations

Affirmations are nothing new and have been well-publicised over the years. By affirmations I mean repeatedly saying your new belief to yourself, over and over again, either out loud or in your head. This might sound a little odd to begin with but it has been proven that saying or writing down your new beliefs is an excellent way to create a new pathway in the brain. For example, if your new belief is 'I am attractive', you could commit to saying this ten or fifteen times in a row, three times a day. It might sound like quite a chore but don't be put off, there are lots of ways you can do this. It's also important to point out that you don't actually have to say your affirmations out loud; you can always do it in your head, which of course makes it easier depending on where you are. I tend to chant my affirmations in the car because I'm normally alone and can say them as loudly as I want to. You might repeat your affirmations in the shower, in the bath, before you go to sleep, before you get up, when you're ironing, washing or gardening, the list is endless. When you really think about it, there are plenty of opportunities throughout your day to integrate this new routine. The most important thing is to put some emotion behind the affirmations, feel what it actually feels like to be living that affirmation. Without the emotional connection your affirmations won't be effective. It's vital for your affirmations to become part of your routine in order for them to work – just like cleaning your teeth. If you find chanting your affirmations a bit dull, how about singing them? Make it fun, not monotonous. Think what would work best for you? One of my clients created a list of the new beliefs that she wanted to work on and then produced a recording of her own voice on her iPod*. She would then listen to the recording while she was cooking, ironing and even before she went to bed. Interested? Another really powerful way to do your affirmation is to stand in front of a mirror whilst you're saying them. It is important to keep your affirmation in the present tense and avoid the use of negative words, for example '*Money is now flowing freely into my life*', '*The world is a safe place for me to live in*' or perhaps '*I have lots of friends who enjoy my company*'.

You may find that writing your new beliefs down would work best for you. By this I mean writing your belief on a piece of paper (Post-it* notes are great for this). You might write even your belief down on a blank piece of paper 20 times in a row, similar to doing lines at school. But, for me the best thing is to write my new belief on numerous Post-it* notes and then plaster them all over the house! Well, almost all over: I tend to keep most of them upstairs so the only people who see them are my family and friends. New beliefs tend to raise a few eyebrows! Put them around the bathroom mirror, on the bedside table, inside the wardrobe door, in a personal organizer, on your bank statements and on your computer screen: anywhere where you know you can't miss them.

What's interesting about doing this is that both your conscious and subconscious mind will be picking up these messages, communication is working on two levels. Throughout our day we are unaware of most of the information our brain acquires.

Visualisation

Lastly, let's look at visualisation. Now, visualisation (or using your imagination) is something we've already covered briefly in Chapter 2, but let me expand a little further here. As I mentioned in Chapter 2, visualisation is a powerful tool used by the world's most successful people. It works on the same principal as the methods we've just discussed and is great at creating new neuro-pathways in the brain. I use visualisation as part of my daily routine – not only to conquer limiting beliefs but for many other things as well. The great thing about visualising is that it's relaxing and energising; in fact, it is addictive! It's extremely simple and everyone has the ability to do it.

Close your eyes for five minutes and create a vivid image in your mind's eye of your new belief being part of your life, almost like looking at yourself six months from now, whether that involves enjoying better health, having more confidence, meeting a new lover or finding a new job. While visualising, remember to use vivid images, sounds and smells to make your mental images as real as possible. Be careful not to let any unconstructive thoughts creep in, keep it positive! A great time for visualising is just before you go to sleep or when you are in the shower. You'll be amazed at how powerful it can be when done regularly.

So there you have it. Does one of these methods resonate with you? Which one are you willing to try? Maybe you'd like to create your own unique way. It doesn't really matter; you just need to decide what will work for you. Perhaps you should try each one in turn, or how about trying all three together? Remember, be kind to yourself and give yourself time. Keep your mind firmly locked on the future not in the past, because that's where your power lies!

Recognising your inner dialogue

To help you further on your journey to revealing your limiting beliefs I want to introduce you to two characters in your life. I say 'introduce', but you're probably already very well acquainted. These two characters are with you at all times, morning, noon and night. They are with you at every success and every failure, at every crossroads and with every decision you have ever made, or will ever make, in your life, good or bad.

Ultimately, listening to one character will direct you to the life of your dreams, whereas the other will have you running around in circles and getting nowhere fast.

I call these two characters, your 'Inner Guide' and your 'Inner Critic' but, quite frankly, you can call them whatever you fancy, 'Angel and Devil', 'Light and Dark', 'Tom and Jerry' or even 'Luke Skywalker and Darth Vader'. Identifying the different voices and scripts between these two characters is paramount in helping you to understand your internal dialogue and eventually your limiting beliefs.

Your Inner Critic is loud and aggressive. This is the voice that consistently tells you how stupid you are, how unattractive you are or how unlucky you are. This voice was formed early in childhood as a tool of protection and its job was (and still is) to keep you safe and cosy within your comfort zone, keeping you from any potential harm. For example, if you were bullied at school your Inner Critic formulated the belief 'Don't be different or you'll get picked on'; its job would then be to make sure you live your life in line with this particular belief so that you wouldn't get hurt again. Your Inner Critic simply does its job. It keeps you tied to the confines of your beliefs, finding 'evidence' along the way to support them. The problem is, as we grow up, our Inner Critic is still trying to rule us, even though we have outgrown the beliefs that were formed in our childhood. Living your life ruled by your Inner Critic is a recipe for disaster as it prevents us from moving outside our comfort zone. Unfortunately, most of us live our life governed by this voice alone, simply because no one has ever told us there is another way. But, you'll be pleased to know there is a simple solution, which we'll come to just as soon as we've met the counterpart of the Inner Critic – your 'Inner Guide'.

Your Inner Guide is quite different. The bad news about the Inner Guide is that this character is very softly spoken, so its whispers may be very difficult to hear over the much louder and more aggressive voice of the Inner Critic.

Your Inner Guide comes right from within, from a higher wisdom of knowing, which I call 'gut feeling' or 'intuition'. Once you start to listen to your Inner Guide instead of your Inner Critic your life becomes transformed. The job of your Inner Guide is to keep you true to who you are and to your unique blueprint. It knows what will make you happy and it knows how to get you there – all you have to do is tune in and listen!

The solution is simple: start listening!

Notice which voice is more prominent, and when? Do you find you are spending most of your day listening to your Inner Critic? Do you find the voice is louder when you're in a particular place or with a certain person? If this is the case, it's a clear indication that behind this voice lies a limiting belief of some kind which needs changing. When you hear the negative drone of your Inner Critic, ask yourself 'What limiting belief is my Inner Critic protecting me from?'

For the best results, make it a habit to sit in your favourite chair, or lie on the bed and spend five minutes a day tuning into your Inner Guide. What has it got to tell you? What is its advice? The more you can do this the easier you'll find it to tune into your Inner Guide at any time of the day, no matter what's going on around you.

Exercise

I want you now (in your journal or on a blank piece of paper) to characterise both your Inner Critic and Inner Guide. I want you to describe what both characters are like. Is your Inner Guide like an angel? Or is he or she dressed in casual jeans with a warm smile and a fresh face? Is your Inner Critic a wrinkled old lady with no teeth, or dressed like a traffic warden? Have fun with this. I'm just trying to help you to differentiate between the two characters, or voices, because when you do this, you're half-way there.

Now, answer the following questions.

My Inner Critic
- What is the general conversation of your Inner

Critic? (What type of things does he or she say to you?)

- When do you find your Inner Critic is loudest? (When I discuss money with my partner, when I'm in a meeting with my boss, when I look in the mirror.)
- How does this affect you? (Stops me from progressing my career and becoming successful.)
- What steps can you put in place today to ensure you turn down the volume of your Inner Critic?

My Inner Guide

- What is the general conversation of your Inner Guide? (What type of things does he or she say to you?)
- When you're fearful or scared what does your Inner Guide tell you?
- When you feel like you have failed what does your Inner Guide say to you?
- How can listening more to your Inner Guide change your life for the better?
- What steps can you put in place today to ensure that you start listening more to your Inner Guide?

Here are five ways in which you will know that you have mastered listening to your Inner Guide.

- The decision you have made just feels right.
- You feel relaxed and confident about where you're life is going.
- You feel like life supports you and everything you do feel effortless.
- You trust your gut feeling or intuition even though there seems to be no logic.
- You find yourself having more enthusiasm and energy than ever before.

So, make it your decision today to start noticing which voice you're listening to. Is it your Inner Critic, keeping you in the confines of your own prison, or is it your Inner Guide, guiding you to your ultimate happiness?

Exercise

Spend five minutes a day tuning into your Inner Guide – what has your Guide got to say? What advice does your Guide have for you? Commit to doing this exercise for seven whole days (just five minutes, perhaps in the shower or before you get up or go to sleep) and make a note of any ideas or insights you receive during this time.

How much do you really like yourself?

One thing I quickly came to realise when I starting coaching clients was how little self-worth people actually have for themselves. Most people don't really like themselves at all. Everything you attract into your life is a mirror of what you believe you deserve: jobs, people, and circumstances are all reflections of how you feel about yourself. Just as with our limiting beliefs our self-worth is created very early on in life by those around us.

Having a young daughter myself I'm very aware of what messages she receives and I'm constantly telling her how wonderful, clever, special and beautiful she is. This is quite different from the messages most of us received as youngsters. Some of you might think I am setting up my daughter for a fall in later life, but I disagree. I want her to have the highest degree of self-worth possible because I know that if she's truly loves herself she will never need look outside herself to others to make her feel fulfilled or appreciated. When we dislike ourselves we are constantly looking for approval from, friends, parents and lovers. I know fully grown adults who are still desperately seeking the approval of their parents! All approval should come from within and not from others; otherwise we spend our whole life desperately seeking endorsement from outside sources.

Loving yourself isn't egotistical or big-headed, that's just fallacy – loving yourself is extremely healthy – and those who do live much more successful lives than those who don't. People who hold positive beliefs about themselves seem to attract more good into their lives, they enjoy more opportunities, money and love and are happier and kinder human beings, on the whole.

Exercise

- On a scale from 1 to 10 (1 being 'not very much' and 10 being 'very much') how much do you like yourself?
- Why have you given yourself this score?
- Where did your beliefs about yourself originate?
- What gets in the way of you loving yourself more?
- What limits do you create by not loving yourself fully?

I think it's fair to say that most of us have some kind of limiting belief about our self-worth; I certainly haven't met anyone who hasn't. But, in the same way that you address a limiting belief using the methods we've talked about, you can also address your level of self-worth and take steps to increase your self-esteem and acceptance. Here's one technique for you to try.

Exercise

Find some quiet time, just five or ten minutes where you won't be disturbed, and stand in front of a large mirror and look at yourself face-on. Take a couple of deep breaths and relax.

I want you to look into your own eyes and tell yourself 'I love you'. Notice how your body reacts to this message: you may feel the need to look away, you may even feel tearful or you may hear your Inner Critic dismiss this positive statement, replacing it with something negative. Doing this exercise can feel very odd and uncomfortable to begin with because we spend our entire lives scolding ourselves rather than using words of love and praise. By doing this exercise you are releasing old negative beliefs and reprogramming your mind with more positive messages that will enable you to truly love yourself.

Repeat the statement 'I love you' enough times for you to be able to fully accept it. You can also repeat any positive statement or affirmation to yourself, such as 'I truly accept myself for who I am' or 'I am healthy and my body is filled with energy'.

I suggest you do this exercise for a few minutes every day; make it a habit, just like brushing your teeth, and notice the difference it makes over a month.

Exercise

Answer the following questions.

- Write down five things that you like about yourself?
- Write down three things that make you totally unique as a person?
- Write down three things for which you are grateful about yourself?

Put your answers somewhere you will be reminded of them often!

Lifting off the layers

Uncovering limiting beliefs really is just the first step on your journey to self-discovery, but, in my eyes, it's the most important part. You need to know what you believe about yourself and the world around you in order to point your life in the right direction. Take one step at a time. Challenge your beliefs. Peel off one layer at a time and that way it won't feel so uncomfortable. Just when you think you've cleared away one belief another one will appear, but that's OK. Think of it as de-cluttering your house or weeding your garden: you may well have a mad blitz initially, but you know it's inevitable that you're going to have to keep on top of it. It's a never-ending journey. You need to keep de-cluttering and you need to keep weeding. Accept that that it's all part of life's course, part of your unique journey. The more you let go of your limiting beliefs the happier you'll become and the more true to yourself you will be. You'll have the courage, perhaps for the first time in your life, to experience new things, to meet new people and to create a life beyond your wildest dreams! But it all depends on you. Nobody is responsible for your life but you, and once you really and truly accept this, you have won power back! With this power you will then have the ability to create miracles.

Jonathan's story

Here is a short story about Jonathan and how he tackled his limiting beliefs in order to have a successful and loving relationship.

Jonathan's goal was to meet someone special. He'd had a few serious relationships and unfortunately they hadn't worked out for one reason or another. His confidence was at an all-time low and he needed some help. He found that he kept attracting the same type of girl over and over again, and he realised that something needed to change.

Whilst Jonathan seemed to be unlucky in love he was hugely successful in all his career endeavours. He worked for an information technology (IT) firm and had enjoyed numerous promotions over recent years, leaving him in a senior managing role on a very comfortable salary.

We talked extensively about his self-limiting beliefs and his behaviour, and it was apparent to both of us that every time Jonathan met someone new he expected the relationship to fail. He became more and more needy and possessive, and because of this, he became convinced that every relationship he entered would fail. Subconsciously, he would then sabotage the relationship in whatever way he could. And, of course, it worked every time and the cycle went on and on. Deep down Jonathan knew this, but what he needed was help to turn things around.

We started by defining what Jonathan actually wanted from a partner: honesty, integrity, humour, and so on, and moved on to established his boundaries: what was acceptable to Jonathan and what wasn't. Once we had done the groundwork Jonathan felt much more confident and aware of what he was looking for in a relationship. We then moved on, physically and mentally letting go of old baggage. Jonathan cleared out his cupboards removing memorabilia from ex-girlfriends, which he no longer needed. Finally, we moved on to addressing Jonathan's self-worth and limiting beliefs. He started doing affirmations and visualisation work regularly. Daily Jonathan would stand in front of the mirror and repeat his positive affirmations to himself. Each night he would also spend a few minutes imagining sharing his life with someone special, how his life would look and how he would feel.

Jonathan continued to do this for many months, and had numerous dates in the process. Eventually he did meet someone special and he is now happily married with his first child on the way.

Chapter 4

A new way of thinking

In this chapter I'd like to introduce you to a fascinating concept that will undoubtedly stretch your thinking further, taking you out of your comfort zone into unfamiliar territory. When I found out about this concept my life changed overnight, and things have never really been the same since. I want you to read this chapter with an open mind and heart, as what I'm about to share with you has the potential to change your life immediately in unimaginable ways.

Your hidden power

What would you say if I told you there was a hidden power within you that had the potential to create a world you wanted to live in: a world of greater prosperity, happiness and peace? Would you think I had gone bonkers or was living in 'la-la' land?

Probably: I can't blame you if you did. But I can assure you I'm not bonkers and I am definitely not living in 'la-la' land. In fact, my feet are well and truly rooted in the ground for the first time in my life.

I'm sharing this with you because once you discover this inner power it has the ability to change your life beyond belief – and I'm not being all 'airy-fairy' here. I mean it will change your life in unthinkable ways.

There is power running through your body, causing your heart to beat, your blood to flow, your cells to regenerate and your hair to grow. A life force energy, with such effect that all these things happen effortlessly and without our intervention. This immense power makes our lives possible, and enables you to read these words; it not only makes you tick, it makes all life possible everywhere. In fact, this power is exactly what thrust this very book into your hand! This power is known as the 'Law of Attraction'.

This law, just like the law of gravity, has been around since the year dot. Only now is science starting to recognise and appreciate its importance, and hence publicise it to the world. As a consequence, many people are now waking up to this intriguing law and instigate its principles into their lives.

I first stumbled upon the Law of Attraction after the birth of my daughter. A friend with whom I worked at the time came bouncing into my office early one Monday morning beaming from ear to ear. She produced a bright orange book from under her arm and shoved it into my hand with very little explanation, saying, 'You must read this!' I was a little bemused to say the least, but promised her I would take a look.

This bright orange book sat unread on my kitchen work surface for almost three weeks before the obligation to read it made me pick it up. But in two chapters this book had not only captivated me, it had thrown my life upside-down (in a good way). It had turned my version of reality on its head and opened a door in my mind that had been locked shut since the day I was born. My life would never be the same again, and deep down I knew it – I had felt an enormous shift.

So what is the Law of Attraction and what could possibly have such a profound effect on my life? Well, let me begin by telling you what the Law of Attraction states: *your thoughts and feelings create your reality – every thought you think, no matter how trivial you might believe, has an impact on your world.*

Philosophers have been telling us this for thousands of years: what we think, we become. Science has proved that our thoughts and feelings really do create our reality. Let me repeat that.

Your thoughts and feelings create your day-to-day life, all the good and the bad. Nobody is responsible for your life but you!

Most of us, however, rarely make the connection between the trend of our thoughts and the way our lives work, so when someone tells us the cause of our troubles is our thinking we brush it off as nonsense. But, if you look hard, you can see it working not only in your own life but also in the lives of all those around you.

We are always creating!

Think about it! Everything you think about in your mind will eventually become your reality.

Have you ever wondered why some people have it all? Happiness, money, love, the perfect job, freedom… What is it that they do differently from you? Consciously or unconsciously, they use the power of their thinking to create a wonderful life! I know for certain that changing your life by changing your mind works. I know, because I've done it. Whether you're devoutly religious, deeply spiritual, an atheist, are agnostic or simply sceptical, the reason I became a life coach is because I want you to know just what a powerful creator *you* are, and show you how to start using this power to your advantage.

You are a human magnet!

Let me explain further. Every thought you have vibrates at a certain frequency, it is then broadcast out into the universe and attracts all things that are vibrating at that same frequency. Therefore whatever you give off simply comes back to you like a boomerang, whether it is good or bad. The truth is, every hour of every day we have the ability to create our life the way we want it to be, from attracting our dream job to solving our global pollution problems. No one lives beyond this Law just as no one lives beyond the law of gravity. It's just that until recently we never realised that it applies to you and me.

The Law is impersonal; it doesn't judge or punish you it simply plays back to you what you send out. The law of gravity isn't personal, it doesn't decide one day it will work for you and next it won't – thank goodness! The Law of Attraction is no different, it's just energy doing 'its thing', doing what it's always done since the dawn of time. We have laws of physics, the law of nature and the Law of Attraction! No one lives beyond this Law and it is behind every success or failure in our lives. We are literally walking magnets, constantly attracting into our experience anything that is on our frequency.

Science is going through some remarkable changes at present as we continue to understand more about how the universe works. At the forefront of these exciting changes is quantum physics. In rudimentary terms, quantum physics is the study of small particles of energy. Now, I'm no scientist and therefore am not qualified to explain the inner workings of quantum mechanics, so I'm going to leave that to those who are far more qualified. All we really need is to learn how to apply this Law of Attraction to our everyday lives. So, do we really need to know the science behind the Law of Attraction? In my eyes: no. I know when I press the button on my central heating controller the house gets warm. Do I need to know the ins and outs of how my boiler works? Not really, not unless I want to become a gas fitter, and I don't. Nor do I want to become a quantum physicist. But, for those of you who need a little dose of science to help you understand the concept, the study of quantum physics is where you'll find your answers.

If we understand the concept of the Law of Attraction we can start to use it to our advantage, just like switching on the central heating to warm our house.

OK, so let me ask you this: What is it you're expecting to happen in your meeting with your boss? What are you expecting the traffic to be like when dropping the kids off at school? What are you expecting to see when you look in the mirror? What are you expecting to see when you look at your bank statement? What you are expecting to happen in your life?

If your answer to these questions is 'The same as always' I've made my point: this is the Law of Attraction being demonstrated in your life. If you think and believe the same thing, day in and day out, you will continue to experience the same things in your life. You get what you expect!

Your thoughts are energy. And your life is like a holographic image of the thoughts and beliefs you hold in your head. The movie screen you call your life is created by the thoughts, feelings and beliefs that you hold in your mind. In your everyday natural state you have the ability to manoeuvre your life in the direction you want it to go, from having a happy family life to influencing world peace, simply by changing your thoughts and feelings.

The most important thing to remember is that we actually create by feeling and not by thought. If thoughts are the steering wheel, feelings are the engine that drives the car. We get what we get by the way we feel and not by trying to force things into place or by trying to control the mind. In short, it's not about monitoring every thought in our head (this would be impossible), it's simply about monitoring our feelings and emotions as they are a clear indication of what we are thinking and therefore creating.

If you are worried about money you are sending those thoughts and feelings out into the universe, and the universe will match those vibrations and keep sending you more of the same – more money worries. It's not until you change your thoughts and feelings that your vibrations will change and, in turn, your circumstances will alter as a result. It's the same with your current relationships, your job, your health, your family, your friends, your weight and so on.

When you are feeling happy and joyful you are sending out high-frequency vibrations, and you may be sure that you are attracting good things back into your life. On the flip-side, when you are feeling lousy and consumed with worry or fear you are sending out low-frequency vibrations which are only going to bring you bad things in return. So, whether it's high vibrations of love or low vibrations of fear, whatever you're vibrating at any given moment is what you are attracting back into your life.

Have you ever experienced a day where it just seemed to go from bad to worse? Perhaps you started off in the morning by having an argument with your partner and left the house feeling angry and frustrated. You then got caught in horrendous traffic, so by the time you arrived at work you were really wound up, and from there the day just snowballed. Sound familiar? Why is this? The more sustained negative thoughts and feelings you have, the more highly charged emotions you are sending out into the universe. The universe responds to the vibrations you are giving off and returns more of the same. When I stub my toe or break a glass, it's a gentle reminder to stop and bring my attention to what's going on in my head. It's a reality check – it's the universe's way of saying, 'You're heading in the wrong direction, turn around!'

Two gentlemen in the 1930s tried to prove that thoughts were real things by photographing the vibrations that particular thoughts carried. Not only did they managed to prove thoughts actually did carry different vibrations, they also found that the more emotion with which the thinker/sender charged his or her thoughts the clearer the photograph turned out to be. This was the first experiment that proved that there is magnetic energy attached to our thoughts, and that thoughts are propelled by our emotions. So when you focus on something like your money worries, your continued negative emotions just make the situation get bigger and bigger. The more you think about something with charged emotion, the larger and more intense that something becomes in your life.

We need to wake up to the fact that we are not just flesh and bones we are electromagnetic beings: walking magnets able to attract into our lives whatever we desire by controlling the feelings that are generated from our thoughts.

The mass consciousness

We live on a planet of predominantly low frequency, brought about by over six billion inhabitants who are all vibrating more feelings of stress, worry and fear than feelings of love, joy and peace. This is because most of us spend our entire day listening to our Inner Critic, whose job is to keep us confined to our limiting beliefs. This can make trying to raise our own frequencies or vibrations difficult. Sometimes we can feel down without really knowing why, and it is usually because we're picking up on someone else's negative energy or vibrations. We literally bathe ourselves in unconscious negativity, from things like watching TV, reading the newspapers and mixing with negative people. You know this is true when a negative person walks into a room and you immediately feel the difference in the atmosphere. Conversely, you also feel it when someone positive walks into the room as you pick up on their positive vibes. We've all experienced this at some time or another. Without a doubt, as we go about our daily lives we are picking up unwanted energy from those around us. I have made a vow to myself not to get mixed up in negative conversations or tittle-tattle, read newspapers, gossip magazines or even watch heavy or negative TV programmes like the news because they affect my mood and the way I feel. It doesn't mean I don't care. On the contrary, it just means I'm protecting myself. We need not let outside circumstances, or other people's moods, affect our own. And this means not getting involved in someone else's trauma. As much as we think we're helping, we are actually making it worse not only for ourselves but for the other person as well.

Your life is like a blank canvas on which you may paint whatever picture you fancy. The problem is no one has ever told you that you have complete freedom. So instead you look across at the person at your side and copy them. In doing so you find yourself painting with the same colours and drawing the same pictures over and over again, simply because you knew no different. In truth, you actually have access to hundreds of colours and may paint whatever picture your heart desires. So ask yourself: 'Have I been painting the same picture over and over again?' Maybe now is the time to start painting something new.

The more people who know and understand about the Law of Attraction the more we will begin to see a shift in the mass consciousness on our planet.

Taking responsibility

Take the very first step with the Law of Attraction: understanding. You need to understand and research. Don't take my word for it. Investigate and find out for yourself. On my own journey I have learnt never to take one person's word as gospel. The truth lies within you, right now. It's just a case of finding the right people, teachers, books and workshops to help you to discover your own inner truth. Once you fully understand the Law of Attraction move on to responsibility. This is the hard bit, as you need to take responsibility for everything that has ever happened in your life – all the good and all the bad.

As you embark on this adventure you soon realise that there are no victims in life. Playing the victim just guarantees unhappiness from the prolonged emission of low vibrations. Accepting liability can be extremely hard for people; some people just find it easier to blame others for their misfortunes. You must take responsibility in order to embrace the concept, and use it to your advantage. The rest of the world will continue to blame their partners, bosses, friends, governments and so on for what is happening in their lives, or will blame their circumstances for their bad luck or even God for punishing them. Please don't judge anyone for coming to this conclusion. I remember being so excited by the realisation that what we send out comes back to us and that we all have the potential to shape our lives exactly how we want, how amazing! It really felt like I had the missing key. But, naïvely, I expected everyone else to be as excited as I was. They weren't! In fact, they just shot me down, and told me I was being ridiculous and outlandish. What I have come to realise is that people's consciousness evolves when they are fully ready to receive. When this will occur is down to the individual, and no amount of convincing or cajoling will change that one iota. Everyone is on his or her own path and exactly where he or she should be for their own evolution. Just because you might believe the Law of Attraction, or anything else, for that matter, don't expect everyone else to do the same because they won't. This is your journey, so stop worrying about others and concentrate on yourself! Realisation comes to everyone eventually.

Right now it's important to realise that no one's asking you to become a goody two shoes all of a sudden – skipping around smiling from ear to ear. Let's get real here. Some days are better than others. Life is about duality. You can't know light unless you know dark. You can't know cold without knowing warm. You can't know sad without knowing happy. This is what life is all about. Please don't expect just because you know all about belief systems and the Law of Attraction that you're never going to experience another bad day. You will, I promise you! From time to time you will stub your toe, have a disagreement with your partner, scratch your car or break a nail. Understanding the Law of Attraction doesn't mean you're exempt from anything bad happening to you, it just means you become more aware of how you're thinking and feeling, and can pull yourself out of any unwanted emotions far quicker than ever before. The Law is simple in concept but practice is necessary to apply it effectively. Like everything you read in this or any other book it will never do you any good until you actually integrate the techniques and advice into your life. It's not enough to 'know it', you have to 'live it' and practise it to fully understand and see the evidence flow into your life.

The magic of 'feelings'

If you don't have what you want in your life right now it's because you are consistently thinking about what is it you don't want, and are spending most of your day listening to your Inner Critic. 'I don't want to be in debt', 'I don't want to be in this relationship', 'I don't want to live here anymore', 'I don't want to be unhappy',

'I don't like my boss', 'I don't want to be overweight', 'I don't want to be ill'. I call it the 'I don't want' syndrome. You spend most of your life thinking about what you *don't* want. Remember, the Law of Attraction takes your predominate thoughts and feelings and gives you more of what you're thinking about. The thing is an awful lot of our thinking is done at a subconscious level and we aren't even aware of it. Most people will swear blind that they never have any negative thoughts whatsoever, yet these are the same people who constantly moan about the weather, the government or the number of speed cameras on the roads, and so on. We have over 60,000 thoughts a day; I wonder how many of those we are actually aware of? Let's be honest, you're never going to be able to monitor 60,000 thoughts a day, it would drive you insane! This is why it's extremely important to become aware of how you're actually feeling. Your feelings tell you what you're thinking, and therefore what you're attracting into your life.

Let me repeat that because it's important: *Your feelings or your emotions tell you what you're thinking and therefore what you're attracting, and they are the most valuable and powerful tool you have in your life.*

It's pretty easy: mastering your 'feelings' is the key to attracting what you want in your life. Your feelings are your gift from above to help you to steer your life in the right direction. Think about it for a second, it's really simple. Your feelings tell you at any given moment, what you're attracting into your experience. Isn't that amazing! You don't have to worry about monitoring every single thought that comes into your head; you just have to concentrate on how you're feeling at any given moment. This is where your Inner Guide comes in; he or she is there to assist you in raising your vibrations by helping you change the way you feel. Feeling good means you're attracting good. Feeling bad means you're attracting negative things.

So ask yourself now: 'How do I feel?', 'Who am I listening to at the moment, my Inner Critic or my Inner Guide?'

Are you feeling good? Are you feeling bad?

It all starts with awareness, and by asking yourself the above questions you have taken the very first steps in organising the future you want. You are the one with all the power and you need to start believing it! You have the ability to change anything in your life because you are the one who chooses your thoughts and feelings every second of every day. No one can do this for you. You are in control. You are in the driving seat.

Remember you are your own fairy godmother!

It's a bit like realising that all of your life you've been driving a car without knowing how to work the controls. You've just done what you thought you ought to be doing, pressing random buttons and hoping for the best. Finding out about the Law of Attraction is like being given the missing instruction manual; except that this instruction manual is really simple. It states: *Follow your feeling and the universe will direct you to your desired destination in the fastest and most harmonious route. Ignore your feelings, and the universe will take you on all sorts of detours, moving you further and further away from your desired destination.*

How do I change the way I feel?

If someone at work upsets you it shouldn't affect the way you feel for the rest of the day. Yes, for a few minutes maybe, but not all day. It's the same with anything: getting a parking ticket, having an argument with your partner, finding out you're overdrawn at the bank, spilling red wine down your favourite white trousers or being let down for a date. By letting something – or someone –

drag you down for longer than it or they should you are throwing power away, and at that point you have stopped steering your 'life car' in the direction you wish to go. Don't do it, don't give your power away!

I'm not saying we should deny all bad feelings; that would be unrealistic. We need to experience negative emotions as much as we need to experience positive ones. As stated earlier, life is about duality; we need to know light to know dark and hot to know cold. But when you do find yourself feeling down, change your mood by changing your thinking. Don't stay in a negative place for too long because it's just bringing you more of the things you don't want. It's also important to point out that just because someone has embarked on a spiritual journey doesn't mean they won't get fed up from time to time, come on! We're living a human experience, and yes we'll have good days and bad days, and yes sometimes people will irritate us. Life is about making our experience as pleasurable as possible, and that means being happy. We can achieve this, first, by monitoring our thoughts and feelings.

So don't beat yourself up if you experience negative emotions, they are part of being human. Take them as a signal that you need to change your mood, and tune in to your Inner Guide. How do you change your mood? Well, it's unique for every individual. You need to find what works for you. What you're looking for is something which will shift your thinking away from the unwanted situation and change the way you're feeling in an instant. I call them 'mood-shifters'. Perhaps they may be a secret list of things to help put you back on track when you're feeling negative or downbeat.

Exercise

Create a list of mood-shifters that you think will work best for you. Write your list in your journal or on a blank piece of paper and when you're feeling down you may refer to it to lift you back up again. Here is an example list to aid your thinking:

- Past memories, such as childhood, wedding day, holidays.
- Your children and funny things they say and do.
- Your family pets.
- Your home, your garden.
- Special events that are coming up.
- Special places you like to go.
- People you love.
- Your favourite music.
- Nature.
- Your favourite hobby or pastime.

When I first started doing this I remember typing and laminating a list of all my mood-shifters, and when I found myself feeling less than happy I would go and sit in the ladies (at work mainly), read through my list, close my eyes and think about each one for a few seconds – it worked wonders for me! Some days I found myself sitting there quite a lot and other days less so.

You need to find what works for you. It might seem like too much effort to begin with, but, believe me, it's not and more importantly it is worth it! It just becomes second nature and just like we outlined earlier, it's just a matter of re-programming the mind. So, yes, at first it feels a little odd, but within a matter of weeks or months you'll be changing any unwanted negative emotions into positive ones in a jiffy.

Another exercise to try is to programme your day in advance. Instead of letting the day control you, why not take hold of the controls and create the sort of day you would like to experience instead.

Exercise

Do this each morning before you start your day. It only takes a couple of minutes and may be done whilst in the shower or getting dressed.

- Find somewhere you can relax, perhaps a favourite chair or by lying on the bed. Make yourself comfortable, and start breathing in and out deeply until you feel your body relax. When you're ready close your eyes.

- Take note of all the wonderful things you already have in your life, from your comfortable home, friends, family, your health or your material possessions. Note everything which you're grateful for, big or small. Leave nothing out!

- Now, imagine another 'you' standing in front of you. This is your true self, the real you! Now notice how your authentic self stands, talks and moves. Notice the confidence that oozes out of your true self and how relaxed and comfortable your other self is.

- Imagine stepping into your true self's body. So your two bodies now become one. Notice the difference it makes to your confidence and the way that you feel.

- Visualise carrying out your day living in the body of your true self: today you are going to be the real you! See yourself doing all your normal activities and talking to your family, friends and colleagues. See how wonderful your day is and how smoothly it runs. Notice how confident you are and how happy you feel. Take a couple of minutes to plan exactly how you want your day to go.

- Open your eyes and bring your awareness back to your surroundings. Don't forget, have a wonderful day!

The power of appreciation

Appreciation is another great tool to help lift those good old vibrations. Being grateful will guarantee that you bring more wonderful things into your life. I remember first finding out about 'appreciation' and thinking 'How on earth can I feel appreciation for something that I don't like?' But I was missing an important lesson. Without feeling appreciation or gratitude for the things you currently have in your life you fail to live in the moment. In fact, you miss it completely. Feeling appreciation is the most powerful way to make you feel better in the moment. So before you start your day thank the heavens for exactly where you are in your life, thank the heavens for manifesting more good into your life, thank the heavens for the day ahead, thank the heavens for the people with whom you will share your day, thank the heavens for the food on your plate, for the car you drive, your children, your partner, your job and so on. The list goes on and on. We all have things to be thankful for. Each and every one of us! Feeling appreciation naturally raises your vibrations without you having to really think about it. If you get stuck finding things to be grateful for, ask your Inner Guide for help. Be grateful for what you have *now*, and start looking at the world through different eyes, through the eyes of appreciation. Appreciate the beauty of nature, appreciate your family, appreciate your boss for paying your wages, appreciate life and – more than anything – appreciate you for being you, as you are unique and there is simply no one else like you. *Nobody does you better!*

Since I started my own journey of self-discovery, cultivating my beliefs and practising the Law of Attraction daily, the one thing that has changed is my ability to appreciate my life fully. Whereas beforehand I was always the first to find the negative in a situation, now, I'm the first to notice the beauty. I am utterly grateful for everything in my life. I haven't necessarily got everything I could possibly want or desire, but I am grateful for what I currently have and not a day goes by when I don't thank heaven for all the wonderful things I have in my experience: my children, my husband, my family and friends, my beautiful home, my garden, the town in which I live, my car, my daughter's school, my local shops, the supermarket delivery man, the food in my fridge, my wardrobe, my cosy bed, my lovely warm pyjamas. And that's just the tip of the iceberg. There is no end of things to be thankful for in anyone's life.

I recently spent the weekend at a health farm (Christmas present from family) and I was sitting contently by myself in the restaurant having my breakfast. While I was dining three middle-aged women came and sat at the table next to me. Within seconds I could hear them moaning about the dirty tablecloth and that one of the seats felt wet. I glanced down at my tablecloth; mine looked perfectly clean. I then heard one of the women complaining that they only had brown bread not white (bearing in mind they had come into the restaurant ten minutes before the end of service). Then the same woman chastised the waitress for taking her empty plate away before she had finished eating. Their conversation was just a barrage of negativity. As I sat there I couldn't believe what I was hearing. Here we all were, at this beautiful spa, being waited on hand and foot when others in the world are dying of hunger and this lady couldn't see just how blessed she was. So what if there was a mark on the tablecloth or if there was only brown bread, it wasn't the end of the world! Remember, you get what you believe, so the more this lady picked up on things that dissatisfied her, the more things she started to notice and complain about.

Being grateful is just a skill we need to relearn. Just like re-programming our limiting beliefs, we too can programme ourselves to be more appreciative of the things we have in our lives.

Exercise

Think of ten things you can appreciate in your day-to-day life and write them down in your journal or on a blank piece of paper. Your list might look something like this:

- I appreciate my beautiful garden.
- I appreciate my good health.
- I appreciate the help my mother gives me with the kids.
- I appreciate my secure job.
- I appreciate this book for helping me on my journey.
- I appreciate my cosy warm bed.
- I appreciate my reliable car.
- I appreciate my partner for his/her love and support.
- I appreciate the town in which I live for all its amenities.
- I appreciate me for being who I am.

Look at your appreciation list when you're feeling down; it is yet another tool you may use to raise your vibrations. Why not read through your appreciation list just before you go to bed each night – what a great way to end each day!

So what if nothing seems to change your mood?

If, for whatever reason, you find yourself completely immersed in negativity and you really can't shift from the pessimistic place you've found yourself in, I have a trick up my sleeve.

Energy wants to move because in its natural state that's what energy does – it moves. When you feel negative it is because you are retaining energy that wants to travel in and out of your body. Your body doesn't want to retain energy; its job is to act as a conduit through which energy flows. It's only when you stop energy from passing through your body that you create all sorts of problems for yourself, including physical ailments; this is why stress is such a killer! We do this unconsciously. By prolonging negative thoughts and feelings we simply stop the energy from moving, the more we hold on to negative thoughts and feelings, the more the energy builds up and the worse we feel. Sometimes people suppress negative energy, such as guilt, anger or an inability to forgive, for years and years, but at some point the energy must be released: it will re-surface and may do so in many forms. Sometimes it re-surfaces at the most inopportune moments, perhaps when we meet a new lover, when we start a new job or, in the worst-case scenario, prolonged retention of negative energy may even manifest as serious illness. This is the last thing we want!

Make it a priority to ensure you are not holding on to any stagnant energy by using some energy-clearing techniques at the beginning and end of each day. Look at it like this: *feeling miserable is energy's way of telling you to release something that is not serving you!*

Here is a wonderful technique to help shift unwanted negative energy.

Exercise

When you are feeling overwhelmed with negativity, go and sit somewhere quiet for a few minutes, somewhere you know you'll not be disturbed, maybe your car, your bedroom or the dining room, or if you're at work, the toilet will do. I want you to sit, close your eyes and take a few deep breaths. I want you to think of what is currently making you feel down: is it an argument you've had; is it stress from work overload; is it the kids being naughty; or perhaps money worries? What is it that's making you feel miserable? Once you know, I want you to find the emotion behind that particular situation.

By emotion I mean how is the negative situation making you feel: is it anger you're feeling; is it frustration, sadness, emptiness, melancholy, anxiety, worthlessness, loneliness, jealousy, resentment, blame, hatred, bitterness, apathy, boredom or concern – find the emotion that you're currently feeling.

Don't get caught up in the drama of the situation that is causing the unwanted emotion; don't replay in your mind what is making you feel this way. Keep the drama out of your mind, all we're looking for here is the primary emotion.

Once you have found the emotion that is causing your unhappiness, take a deep breath and absorb yourself in feeling this emotion. For example, if you've had a really bad day, have had numerous arguments with your partner and you've outlined that the primary emotion you're experiencing is frustration, I want you to immerse yourself in the feeling of frustration.

It might sound like a complete contradiction to what we've been discussing so far, but bear with me.

Make sure you don't replay the arguments in your mind, that's not what we're looking for; ensure you keep concentrating on feeling the frustration only. If your mind strays into the drama again, bring yourself back. Feel the feeling. Feel it!

Absorb your whole body in this feeling, allow yourself to let it rise to the surface. It can do you no harm; it's just emotion. Stay with the sensation until you find the intensity lift, it might take 10 seconds, it might take 30 seconds, it might take longer, just keep feeling the emotion until you feel it lift, or you find yourself getting bored. What you're doing is experiencing the emotion so you can release it. You're discharging any built-up or stagnant energy you've been retaining. Once you've released the energy by doing this exercise, you'll find the frustration has disappeared. Gone! You'll have moved any trapped energy that was causing you to feel the way you were. Remember, energy doesn't want to be trapped, it wants to move!

To recapitulate:

- Find somewhere quiet and peaceful to sit or stand for a few minutes.

- Find out what's bothering you: is it your boss, the kids, the messy house?
- Uncover the primary emotion connected to what's bothering you.
- Absorb yourself in feeling just the emotion for a few minutes until you feel the energy shift.
- Take a deep breath and carry on with your day.
- Practise this exercise as many times as necessary throughout your day (normally once or twice is enough).

We've been taught, especially as children, that it's bad to experience negative emotions. We shout at our children for getting angry, we try to hold back the tears when we're feeling upset and the one about 'men don't cry' is a classic. As human beings we need to experience the whole array of emotions that we were born with. We need to let our children get angry and have tantrums if necessary, all they are really doing is releasing blocked negative energy, such as anger or frustration, and that's completely healthy. I'm not saying don't instil discipline; on the contrary, I am saying we should permit our children learn to express their feelings. Being taught to retain negative emotions is not healthy and it does us more harm in the long run; it can create all sorts of beliefs and odd behaviours in our adult lives. So if you you're feeling angry, frustrated or sad, go hit a pillow, scream out loud, have a good cry and let it all out. You know how good it feels when you cry, that's because you're releasing all your built-up negative energy!

It's important to point out, however, that once you've moved the unwanted energy unless you consciously make an effort to change your thoughts thereafter, the frustration or whatever emotion you're experiencing will return. Once you've done this exercise, make sure you make every effort to stay in a positive frame of mind. Use your mood-shifter list, or whatever works for you, or you'll end up doing the exercise again and again.

I suggest you do this exercise only if you've tried everything else to lift your mood, including your mood-shifter list. If you don't release negative energy you will continue to experience the feeling or the emotion and, through the Law of Attraction, your prolonged negative feelings will bring more of what you don't want into your life.

How to manifest your dreams

OK, so now you know the importance of being in tune with your feelings and how to change your mood and keep it on the up; how do you start to manifest your desired future or goals?

There are many techniques, and 'manifesting' is a huge topic at the moment. I can only speak from my experience and I will share the tried and tested techniques that I have used for many years and continue to use to this day.

The first step in the process of manifesting your dreams is deciding what you actually want (i.e. setting your goals). Now this sounds simple, but if you are not absolutely clear about what you really want, the Law of Attraction cannot bring it to you. You will send out mixed vibrations and will therefore receive mixed results. Unfortunately this is what most of us have been doing all our lives. Very few of us ever set ourselves *measurable* goals and then we wonder why we are still doing the same thing, year in and year out. You need to take control. Remember, the universe is just picking up on your predominant thoughts and feelings, and replaying them back into your life. Your commands are not questioned: what you send out immediately begins to pull people, circumstances and events back into your life to match your 'vibration frequency'.

You need to be very clear about what you want from your future. By becoming clear about your goals you are sending out clear and concise messages. The universe can then get to work in bringing your goals into your experience.

This leads me on to the second step in the process of manifesting – believing and trusting. Once we have a clear mental picture of the things we want we need to trust that the universe has our request in hand. Our only job thereafter is to continue to keep our vibrations up by feeling happy, and not to try and force things to happen, as this is where most of us go wrong. The more we can continue to keep our vibrations up, the faster our goals will manifest into our lives without us having to make much effort at all.

For example, if you received a call from your mum and she announces that she has won a windfall on the lottery and that she'd like to share some with you – you would start rejoicing immediately. You trust your mum implicitly, she's always kept her word and you know she will give you the money – you have no reason to doubt her. You don't wait until the money is in the bank and the cheque has cleared before you start celebrating, or before you thank your mum.

Another example: when you place your grocery order online you know your request is being dealt with; you have no reason to think otherwise. You know it will arrive, so you relax.

These are two examples of how you *feel* when you know your goals will manifest. You need to start believing!

Once you have placed your 'order' with the universe you need to trust that the universe will sort it out for you. You need to believe it's on its way in exactly the same way you would trust your mum with the lottery money or the supermarket with your grocery order. Don't worry, fret or think about your lack – you need to trust in the process. You need to think, act, feel and speak as if your goal is on its way to you, it's inevitable. Now the universe isn't daft, we can't fool it (oh, how I wish we could), if you're continually thinking 'It hasn't arrived yet' the message will be transmitted and you will continue to attract more 'lack'. If you believe you have your manifested goal already the universe will move people, events and circumstance to bring into your experience at record speed.

OK, how do you trust something without prior experience, and how do you start to believe you have achieved your goals already?

First, trust is something you earn over time, but like everything you have to start somewhere. So to make it easier start by trying to manifest something small, like an extra £20 to buy yourself that scarf you saw last week, or how about manifesting a nice cup of tea or a big fat kiss. Start small. Build up trust in the process and then move on.

As for believing that your goals are already manifest, you need to start using your imagination! Do you remember being a child and role-playing? Yes? Well this is what you need to start doing again. And, of course, it's been a while since we all did this, but it is tremendous fun! You could also try doing affirmation or practise visualisations.

Here are some techniques you can try to help you start believing.

- *Vision board*: go and buy a cork pinboard and start cutting out and collecting images or items you see in magazines or in your day-to-day life – pictures of your perfect man, house or something that represents good health or love. Make you vision board colourful and happy, and put it somewhere prominent. Every time you look at it, it should invoke a warm and happy feeling.

- *Role-play*: have an imaginary conversation with yourself (the car's a great opportunity to do this). Talk as if you were having a conversation with your friend telling them about your success having now achieved your goals. What you're doing is jumping into the future and pretending your goal has already manifested. I love this one and do it all the time!

- *Affirmations*: as discussed earlier, do daily affirmations such as 'Money is flowing freely in to my life' or 'My dream man is on his way to me right now'. Have fun with it!

- *Visualisation*: Spend ten minutes a daydreaming about your future. Let nothing negative in, just dream about how your life will be once your goal has manifested into your life.

You could even do all four and manifest your goals at lightning speed!

So we've talked about getting clear on what you want and how to start believing it is already yours. What comes next?

Letting go and receiving. This is where most people tend to give up or come unstuck. We decide what we want, we send that request off into the universe, we start to believe it's on its way and then we get bored or disillusioned and end up going back to our old ways. When we don't see instant results we start trying to force things to happen or try to work out exactly how they will happen and in doing so we get in the way of the universe bringing it to us. Allow the universe to do it for you! Whilst we are trying to work out how it will all happen we are sending out a vibration of lack of faith, and hey, you've got it, the universe will simply bring us more lack of faith. It is just playing back what we are sending out. So once we have decided what we want it really is paramount that we let go and trust implicitly that it's on its way to us.

You may struggle with this and find it almost impossible to 'let go'. You may send your 'order' out there and then 30 seconds later wonder why it hasn't arrived yet. You may find yourself trying to make things happen or forcing things into place. The result: it will blow up in your face. If you don't let the universe do its job you will get in the way and sabotage your desires because you didn't trust that the universe would deliver them. One of the biggest lessons in life is learning to *let go*. From time to time, when you feel fearful for whatever reason, you will fall into this old trap and start trying to control everything again. When you let go amazing things start to happen, things you could have never dreamt or created yourself. Over the years you will learn to have more trust that all will work out exactly as it should.

Once we have learnt to let go we need to become fully open to receiving. We need to keep our eyes and ears open for signs and hints of our goal getting closer to us. We need to remember to tune into our Inner Guide as much as possible. The more we continue to feel good and believe, the faster our goals will manifest. So what you're looking for are little signs in your day; it might be a brainwave that comes to you in the shower; it might be an e-mail or a call, or something you find on the internet, or maybe someone you speak to. You need to remain open to the signs that the universe is giving you! Believe me they are there.

It's important to point out that although we live in a wonderful and magical world, we are still living in a physical reality and therefore we still need to take physical action. The difference though is that the action you decide to take will be action derived from your gut feeling or intuition, and not from your logical mind. There is a huge difference. It's a bit like going for a walk on an extremely windy day. When you're walking with the wind coming towards you, you get buffeted and blown about, it feels uncomfortable, cold and takes much longer to get where it is you want to go. On the other hand, if you walk with the wind behind you it carries you along and your journey is much more pleasant. The same applies to following your intuition. If it flows effortlessly, and feels good in the process, you know you're on track, but if it feels like you've got a hurricane in your face it may be time to consider turning around and going in the opposite direction. Feels good? You're on track. Feels bad? You're not.

Sometimes people get put off by the word 'action' as they think it implies hard work, but life shouldn't feel this way if you're heading in the right direction; it should feel effortless! Yes, some days will seem a little harder than others, but as a whole your journey should be a pleasant ride. I remember one particularly large goal I was working on a few years back; it wasn't until I'd achieved my goal that I became surprisingly aware of how effortless my journey had been from start to finish. It didn't feel like I'd taken much action at all, because it was so natural, easy and uncomplicated. I knew for sure that there was no way I could have figured out my path using just my logical mind alone. Nearly all the actions I'd taken had come from my gut or intuition. It really is amazing when everything just flows with minimal involvement from us!

If you can let go and be open to receiving you will simply attract everything you need to manifest what you desire. If it's a certain website you need you'll find it; if it's people you need you will be attracted to them; if it's money you're short of you'll attract it; if it's a new home you'll find it; if it's a new job you'll get it. You will attract everything, and I mean everything, you need in order to fulfil your dreams or desires. When the opportunity presents itself, when you get that impulse to do something, or when you get that moment of clarity or insight, follow it! If it feels right, act. Don't delay, don't try and to be too logical. Take one little step at a time and before long you will have reached your destination.

Everyone can do this; you don't have to be special, gifted, educated or rich. We all have the ability to attract what we want. The only difference is that some of us choose to take responsibility for our lives and some of us don't. Now you have the knowledge, which option will you choose?

Remind yourself how to manifest your goals

- Decide want you want. Set your goals. Get completely clear about what you desire from your future. Make sure it's something you really want and not something someone else wants you to do or be. It's time to get selfish.
- Let go. Don't try and figure it out or control the outcome.
- Trust and believe the universe is working behind the scenes to bring your order to you.
- Keep your vibrations up by feeling happy, positive and grateful.
- Receive. Look out for all the signs and signals the universe presents to you.
- Take action. Make sure the action feels good, that way you know you're heading in the right direction.

Your belief system and the Law of Attraction

Once you start working with the Law of Attraction you will sometimes find that some things are easier to manifest than others. For example, you might find it really easy to manifest a parking space or a new outfit yet trying to manifest more money into your life seems near impossible! Why? When you come up against this problem you need to take a step back and look at your programming. By this I mean your limiting beliefs. Do you remember in the previous chapter we talked about how once we have formed a belief we will continue to live our lives by the rule of that particular belief, finding evidence along the way to support it? If you find the Law of Attraction isn't working in a particular area of your life, such as money, you need to look at what your underlying beliefs are about wealth and prosperity. If you are running a negative belief of some kind it will stop the universe from bringing your desire to fruition. It all starts with your beliefs. So if you come up against a roadblock, go back and do some of the exercises in Chapter 3. Answer the questions again and set a plan of action to start changing your mind-set. Once you change your beliefs the universe can then deliver the goods. It's that's simple.

How long does manifesting take?

A lot of this has to do with how many limiting beliefs you hold. The fewer you have, the easier it is to get the Law of Attraction to work for you. This is why I talk so extensively about your programming; this is where the journey must start. The more you believe in the Law of Attraction the faster your manifestations will appear in your life. Theoretically, if you think about it, the universe doesn't see things as big or small. Everything is energy, therefore manifesting £10 should be no harder than manifesting £1000; it is just our human collective belief that £1000 must be harder to attract, simply because we deem it to be worth more. This is something we have been taught – it doesn't mean it is necessarily true. Again, it all boils down to a matter of belief. Do you believe it's harder to manifest £10 than £1000? If you believe it, so be it. Expectation is a powerful thing. My advice to you is to start by trying to manifest small things, like £5 or a parking space. Once you can see the Law of Attraction working for you on a small scale you can use your ability and new-found belief to move on to bigger things – manifesting your dream career, better health or a new home.

So how long do you think it will take: a week; a month; a year; ten years, or never? You decide. You will get what you expect. Period! This is why it's so important to become aware of your beliefs and how they are affecting your life.

According to Einstein, time is just an illusion. What quantum physics tells us is that everything is happening simultaneously. It is we who think time is linear because we see things happen one after another. We live our lives by the clock. Second after second, minute after minute and hour after hour. Try and be brave here, I know it's a mind-blowing concept, but if you understand that there is no time (well, not as we imagine) you will discover that our desired future already exists. It takes no time for the universe to manifest our goals and the delay is simply caused by our belief about what is possible and what is not.

As you look at your current reality, remember not to feel bad or discouraged. Your current circumstances are simply a result of your past beliefs, thoughts and feelings. So if you're in debt it has been caused by past negative thoughts and feeling. It's the same with relationships. If you always seem to attract the wrong type of person, who breaks your heart, that, too, is a result of your past negative thoughts and feelings. You can start to change this pattern right now. As you begin to monitor your thoughts, using your feeling as a guideline, your will set the wheels in motion and you start to see results. It's like planting a seed in the winter: you need to give it plenty of love and nurture it before you see the first shoots. So keep focused, have faith and, more than anything, else feel happy in the process!

So there you have it. I told you it would get you thinking, didn't I? No one masters the art of manifesting overnight; it takes time, so don't be too hard on yourself. Remember, it has taken your whole life to get where you are now. I'm not saying it will take as long to change things, but you need to be patient. It's like unravelling a ball of wool: there'll be some detangling to do, but in the end it'll be worth – I promise.

Exercise

Write a list of 30 things, either in your journal or on a blank piece of paper, that you want to manifest within the next five years, including the goals you set in Chapter 2.

Your list might look something like this.

- To have perfect health.
- To find a career that really inspires me.
- To meet my ideal partner.
- To write my first book...

Now get manifesting!

Paul's story

Paul was fascinated by the concept of the Law of Attraction and after successfully manifesting small goals he decided he wanted to start manifesting more substantial things. Paul had a considerable amount of debt, including a student loan, which he felt hung over him restricting him from making the life changes he desired.

Paul decided he wanted to attract £25,000, which would pay off all his loans and credit cards, leaving him free to pursue the life changes he dreamt of. First, he took time to write a list of all the things he wanted to attract and he got his girlfriend to write a fake cheque for £25,000, payable to himself and signed by 'The Universe'. Paul stuck this to his bathroom mirror. He wrote a series of notes stating 'money is flowing freely into my life' and put them in various places around the house where he would see them every day. Each morning, while in the shower, Paul would spend a few minutes visualising how £25,000 would change and enhance his life.

Three months' later Paul was head-hunted for a new job in London, with an increased salary of £15,000. Shortly after this he came into a windfall another £3000 from a long-lost relative he'd never even met! OK so Paul didn't attract the full £25,000 but do you think he was bothered? Absolutely not! He has now written himself a new cheque for £50,000.

Chapter 5

Who are you?

Here we are at Chapter 5. I hope you're feeling invigorated, energised and not too bewildered. We've peeped inside the dark crevices of your mind to discover any limiting beliefs which may be lurking there and have exposed how those beliefs may be sabotaging your success. We then delved a little deeper into your psyche to discover how to work with the universe to manifest your dreams. Now it is time for you to get to know yourself at a much deeper level. I mean really get to know yourself – all the things that make you *you*.

Are you ready to come face to face with yourself?

OK, so let's imagine you have cleared out all your old baggage: your limiting beliefs, childish habits and ridiculous behaviours, and you now feel shiny and squeaky-clean. What does that leave you with? Who are you now all those layers have been lifted off?

We have been running our beliefs, habits and behaviours since the day we were able to open our eyes and we lost touch with our blueprint, or authentic self, long, long ago. In fact, we are so convinced of our beliefs, habits and behaviours that once we start to change the patterns we've been running all our lives it may feel as if we have lost the use of a limb.

Suppose this feeling is a fear of the unknown: 'If I don't play the super hero, what on earth will I do with my time?' 'Who will I become?' When you embark on a journey of self-discovery you are committing to change, and in the process letting go of anything that no longer serves you. But in doing so, you determine a new path, a new future and, ultimately, a new you. You need to let go of the old to receive the new. And, believe me, the new you is *far better* than you can possibly imagine. It's a bit like most wardrobes, so crammed with clothes that are no longer worn, which the owner can't squeeze into any more. The clothes overflow to the wardrobe door handles and the owner's partner starts to moan what a mess the bedroom looks. When it gets to this point it's time to de-clutter and throw out the items that are no longer needed – which of course just makes room for some new clothes. It's the same with your life. Letting go, leaves room for new events, situation and people to enter your life. Holding on to someone or something is never any good for us; in fact, it's very damaging because we stop ourselves from receiving more good things. Remember, energy wants to move!

So how do you get to know yourself?

We need to uncover our unique blueprint, which holds within it our personality, talents, passions and the values that make us whom we are. There are people who have a natural talent for making people laugh, for healing or for nature. As we noted earlier, there are those who have a natural talent for creating inspiring works of art, for playing a musical instrument or the ability to sing in tune without effort. It's this differentiation that makes this world such a diverse place in which to live. And we *all* have passions, values and talents. If your Inner Critic is telling you otherwise, tell him (politely!) to shut up until you've finished this section of the book. Each one of us shares the common purpose of contributing something of value to this world by using the unique set of passions, values and talents that we have.

Unfortunately, as also mentioned before, our talents, passions and values are covered up early on in life, when our parents, teachers or friends tell us that 'You'll never be able to do that', 'You're just not clever enough' or 'You can't do that, it's far too expensive'. We accept these restrictions as the limitations of our world and our lives, we drift off course and then we wonder how on earth we came to be in the situation we're in. Our beliefs take over our lives and direct us to destinations we never dreamed of visiting. A strong indication that you are living your life by someone else's rules or beliefs is that you become indecisive and can't make decisions for yourself: when you don't trust your gut feelings and seek out 'expert' advice instead; when you hate shopping for a new outfit because you haven't got a clue what suits you; or you end up going along with everyone else's ideas instead of your own and then come to resent it.

When we follow our unique blueprint it will brings us increased joy and happiness. This blueprint is the fundamental bedrock of whom we are. So if we know what our blueprint is we can start to build a life around it, thereby increasing our overall happiness and joy. It's only when our lives are in conflict with our blueprint that we become discontented and unhappy.

In general, if an area in your life isn't working (such as a job or relationship) it's off balance with your blueprint and this may be an opportunity for you to re-assess things. For example, I could easily have become a maths teacher (at a very basic level), but maths was not a subject I enjoyed, nor was I particularly good at it, so to base a career on it would have been futile. Instead, I decided to create a career I truly enjoyed, which encompassed all my natural talents and abilities. The result: I love what I do and wake up each morning with a spring in my step and passion for the day ahead.

When you uncover your blueprint things fall into place naturally, and you suddenly feel like you're not swimming against the tide any more. Things flow smoothly, they fall into place effortlessly and life becomes enjoyable and easy! Think back to the windy day scenario mentioned earlier: if you feel like you've got a hurricane blowing in your face, it's the universe's way of saying 'You're going the wrong way, turn around!'

I want to share with you how to set about uncovering your own unique blueprint by, first, looking at your values and passions.

Are you ready?

Uncovering your values

The first step to uncovering your values and passions is to find out what it is in life that brings you joy. Once you have figured out what brings you joy, you'll have a clearer picture of the make-up of your blueprint.

Now when I say 'joy' I'm talking about those moments in your life, big or small, when you feel sheer pleasure or bliss (you can't include sex in this exercise – sorry!). Moments when your heart swells with joy, your body bubbles over with love, when you feel totally at peace with yourself or the world, or when you feel exhilarated about something. It's that moment when you think 'I'm *really* happy'. Your Inner Critic may pop up again to inform you that you can't recall any moments of joy or happiness recently. Rubbish, of course you can! If you're struggling to think of instances, you're thinking too hard. A simple 'Thank you' from someone that you opened a door for may be a moment of bliss or peace. We all know that being thanked is a wonderful feeling and can really brighten up our day. I want you to write in your journal or on a blank piece of paper six experiences that have brought you joy or happiness within the last two years.

You really need to take some time to think about this, it's important to reflect on all the things, big and small, that have given you that wonderful warm feeling of pleasure or bliss inside. Go and make yourself a nice cup of tea and spend some time reminiscing. Go on, do it now!

To help you along, here is a list of my own six experiences. As you will see, most of these experiences are actually quite small. They're simple pleasures.

- Sitting by the river on a sunny day with my husband and daughter eating ice-cream.
- Creating balance within my day for all my earthy duties, spending quality time with my family and finding time for 'me' and my own personal development.
- Waking up on a Sunday morning and not having to do anything I don't want to do! (Rare, but great when it happens.)
- Being thanked, whether that's a work, by a friend or in the street!
- Reading a wonderful new book.
- Writing an inspirational article.

Exercise

Now write down your own six experiences.

Experience 1 _____

_____

Experience 2 _____

_____

Experience 3 _____

_____

Experience 4 _____

_____

Experience 5 _____

_____

Experience 6 _____

_____

Once you have your list of six experiences, you need to work out what the underlying value or passion is in each experience. It's very simple, ask yourself what each of your experiences is giving you?

To give you an idea let me share with you each of my six experiences and their underlying values.

- Sitting by the river on a sunny day with my husband and daughter eating ice-cream = Love and Security.
- Creating balance within my day for all my earthy duties, spending quality time with my family and finding time for 'me' and my own personal development = Harmony.
- Waking up on a Sunday morning and not having to do anything I don't want to do! (Rare, but great when it happens.) = Freedom.
- Being thanked, whether that's a work, by a friend or in the street! = Appreciation.
- Reading a wonderful new book = Inspiration or learning new things.
- Writing an inspirational article = Achievement.

I now know that my values are:

- Love and security.
- Harmony.
- Freedom.
- Appreciation.
- Inspiration and learning new things.
- Achievement.

Not just the above experiences give those particular values. For example, achievement may be met in many different ways, and not just by writing an article. It could be baking a cake, running a workshop or even decorating the bedroom. It really doesn't matter what you do to meet your values as long as they are met. The more your values are met, the happier you'll be.

Exercise

Now, write down what your own six values are. Here are some key words to help you along.

Freedom, nature, harmony, appreciation, love, learning, fun, achievement, excitement, balance, variety, advancement, security, peace, loyalty, creativity, friendship, stability, power, variety, spirituality.

Value 1 _____

Value 2 _____

Value 3 _____

Value 4 _____

Value 5 _____

Value 6 _____

Exercise

Now you have worked out your six values, answer the following questions.

- What areas of my life are in conflict with my values currently? (For example, not enough '*me* time' or being in a job where no one ever says 'Thank you'.)
- What needs to happen in order to change this?
- What small step can I make this week to start working towards this change?

This week make it your intention to meet as many of your values as possible. Make a plan of action to do more of the things you enjoy and see what difference it makes to your overall well-being at the end of the week.

Your talents

Alongside our values sit our natural talents: things that we enjoy doing and which come easily to us. Our natural talents often start to emerge in early childhood. When we are children we all instinctively know what we enjoy doing, what comes naturally and what we're good at. It may be building sandcastles or playing with *LEGO*˙, drawing pictures or playing a musical instrument.

It's quite interesting to watch children at play and notice the things which they are naturally drawn to doing in their free time. Some children just love the fresh air and at the first opportunity dart outside to play, some are naturally arty and are always keen to show you their latest picture, whereas others are more academic and may often be found in a corner reading their favourite book or inclined to play a musical instrument.

Unfortunately, as we get older we lose touch with our own natural abilities. Our talents tend to get covered up quite early on in life and many of us have lost touch with them by the time we reach our early twenties. We forget who we are. Many of my clients seem to have lost their way. They've spent 20 years doing an unfulfilling job and have no idea how they actually got there. It happens to so many of us. We fall into a job or career and we plod along for years forgetting about our values and talents, forgetting about who we really are and want makes us tick. But then, years later, we find ourselves lost and without direction. We spend so many years following the crowd that we find ourselves far from home with no idea how to get back.

Well, it's time to reclaim your youth, to remember who you were when you were dancing around the living room performing for your aunties and uncles or when you came in at the end of the day with mud up to your armpits after looking for creepy crawlies. I want to encourage you to bring those feelings back and remember your childhood as best you can. I appreciate it may seem like many moons ago, so how about digging out some old photos to revoke some memories or maybe talking to your family about their recollections to discover what you left behind.

If you can't remember the exact thing you liked doing, just find a substitute. What was it that you enjoyed most about performing in front of your aunties and uncles or getting your hands dirty? Was it being centre of attention or enjoying the natural world?

Exercise

To help you to uncover your natural talents answer the following questions. Remember to be as specific as possible and think back over your entire life and, most importantly, write everything down, no matter how silly in appears to be – don't edit yourself!

- When growing up, what did people say you were gifted at or had a talent for?
- What do you find comes easily to you?
- What makes you excited, animated and lights up your face?
- What enjoyable experience makes you lose all sense of time?
- What are you drawn to doing?
- What would you gladly spend your money on to be able to do?
- What activities would you do if money were no issue?
- What things do you pick up faster than others?
- What do you do which amazes others?
- If you were to ask your family or friend what your natural talents are, what would they say?

Now write down what insights you've had from doing this exercise (For example, 'I used to love swimming but I haven't swum in the last 15 years' or 'I used to enjoy doing arts and crafts at school, yet I now spend all my time working in an office doing admin'.)

If you could define four of your natural talents what would they be? (For example, 'people person', 'creative hands', 'great singing voice', 'fantastic cook', 'good listener'.) If you get stuck listing your four talents, ask your friends, family or partner for help.

Talent 1 _____

Talent 2 _____

Talent 3 _____

Talent 4 _____

Now answer the following questions.

- Is there one special talent that stands out above the others?
- As a percentage, how much of your natural talents are being used in your everyday life?

- How can you start using your natural talents more?
- If you were to make a living using your natural talents, what would you do?

This week make it your intention to use as many of your natural talents as possible. Make a plan of action to do more of the things you enjoy and see what difference it makes to your overall well-being at the end of the week.

Now that you are aware of your passions, values and talents you are further towards uncovering your true self. Most people travel throughout life without really knowing who they are and what drives them. So now you know you need to start building your life around *you*. Start making small changes immediately. The more you can live your life in line with your unique blueprint the happier, more fulfilled and confident you will become.

Your life purpose

'Life purpose' is an interesting topic. Do I think we all have a predetermined purpose that we must discover in order to find fulfilment and happiness? *No!* Sorry if that's not the answer you're looking for, but I believe our purpose here on earth is what we make it. Our true purpose is to be happy. Period! Living a life utilising our talents and fulfilling our values will untimely bring us the happiness we are all subconsciously searching for.

When I first discovered my own values and talents I quickly realised that the job I was doing didn't really fit with what I wanted from a career any more. In fact, it helped me make more sense of why I had become so miserable. One of my most important values is appreciation. I like to feel appreciated, I like to be thanked and valued. The company I was working for at the time had recently been through a buy-out and whilst nothing had changed in terms of the day-to-day running of the business, the management team had been replaced. As nice and smiley as the new managers were, it become apparent that they were quite naïve in regards to dealing with their staff and six months into the takeover, the cracks were starting to show and people were leaving in droves. I had gone from being well-respected and appreciated by the previous management to being viewed as just part of the furniture: the new managers had no understanding of my role and what motivated me. Over time my enthusiasm diminished and I become apathetic and disinterested in my role. My values weren't being met any more. And whilst I wasn't consciously aware of this at the time, subconsciously I knew something was amiss.

Having awareness and a clear definition of my values and talents helped me to re-adjust and point my career back in the direction I wanted it to go. Now, this re-adjusting didn't happen overnight, it was a process which took time, but without this awareness the process probably wouldn't have been so smooth and perhaps would have taken far longer than it did. The great thing about knowing your values and talents is you can use them as a barometer to gauge where you currently are, and where it is you want to go. Let's say you been offered a new job and you're not quite sure if it's right for you. Instead of losing endless nights of sleep, simply ask yourself 'Does this new job meet my values and talents?' Not every job will meet all your values, but what you're aiming for is that it meets at least 80% of them; that way you know you're making the right choice.

Exercise

Write down your values and talents on a piece of paper and put it somewhere you can see it every day – as a reminder to live your life 'on purpose'. Keep your eyes and ears open to new opportunities and when something arises, a new idea, or someone says something that strikes a chord with you, take action and follow your inner guidance. Make it your job from now on to live your life in alignment with your values and talents, and see what remarkable changes accrue

Finding your ideal career

There are many people in the UK today who dislike their job or chosen profession. A recent survey showed that the people in the UK are unhappier than those in any other Western nation. I wonder why? As mentioned, many of us fall into a particular job or career without giving our values, passions and talents a second thought. But how can you build a suitable career without knowing your values, passions and talents? The truth is you can't.

It wasn't until I uncovered mine that I suddenly realised I was in the wrong profession. It was a bit of a shock when I discovered that I hardly used any of my natural talents and very few of my values were being met, but having a greater understanding of what made me tick helped me to see clearly which careers were right for me and which weren't. I then had the clarity to point my working life in the right direction.

Before this chapter draws to a close I want you to take a look at your current line of work and evaluate if you are in the right job for you. If not, investigate what is.

Did you know that an average working week is 48 hours long – and far longer for many people? Many of us spend more time at work than we do at home with our families so it has never been more important to ensure that we enjoy our work. Working shouldn't just be about earning enough to pay the mortgage, feed your family or buy the necessities of life. Of course all these things are essential, but your working life should be fulfilling, rewarding and enriching. Having a job that provides all of these things nurtures the soul. There is nothing more gratifying than feeling like your making a contribution the world, whether that's working on a supermarket checkout, in an office or volunteering to work with sick and infirm. On this planet we should all help others by utilising and sharing our unique talents.

So let me ask you an important question: 'Do you enjoy your line of work?'

Be honest with yourself. Just because your job pays well, provides flexitime, gives you 30 days' holiday, a good pension, health insurance, company car and an easy commute does not mean that it is fulfilling, rewarding and enriching. You're fooling yourself, it just means you're comfortable and probably too scared to even dare consider making a move for fear of losing these privileges. If you're in the right job you should wake up in the morning with a spring in your step knowing that today you're going to make a difference the world and add value in some way.

So let me ask you again: 'Do you *really* enjoy your job?'

Exercise
Answer the following seven questions.

- Which of my talents are currently being used in my current job?
- Which values are being met in my current job?
- Three things I hate about my job are?
- Three things I love about my job are?
- How do I feel about going to work every day?
- Three things I would love to change about my job if I could?
- Out of 10, how good is my work–life balance at the moment?

By answering these questions you should be starting to get a clearer picture of whether you're in the right profession or not. Just because you have revealed that your job isn't providing you with the fulfilment your soul is yearning for does not always mean you have to run out and find a new occupation or retrain to do something else. It's not as clear-cut as that. For some a total career change is absolutely the right thing to do, but for others it's just a case of making a few small changes, such as re-addressing your working hours, working from home one day a week, having a pay increase, moving desks or relocating to another office closer to home. Small changes can make a world of difference. So look at your answers to the above questions again. Is it just a few small changes that are required or is it total career shift?

One of my clients was worried that she was in the wrong profession. She was scared that she'd spend eight years training only to find out it wasn't the career for her and she was terrified of what her family and friends would think if she gave it all up. When we started looking at her values and talents it became apparent that it wasn't the actual job itself that was the problem, her work–life balance was throwing her off kilter. All that was required was to make some small changes to her working day. We decided that because she was constantly watching the clock every five minutes, stressing herself unnecessarily, she would leave her wristwatch at home and remove the clock from the office wall. We also decided that instead of working through her lunch break, which she did every day, she would ensure she took a break at least three times a week. She also started walking to work and took up some other activities in the evenings. When I spoke to the client two weeks later the change was phenomenal, she was a much brighter, happier and content person. That's all it took!

But for those of you who know deep down that no matter how many changes you make to your job it will never be right for you, it's time to get clear about what you do want to do.

But I don't know what I want to do!

Career changes are probably one of the most common topics I'm faced with as a life coach. Clients tell me they're unhappy doing what they're doing, but have no idea what they want to do instead.

Deep down if we're completely honest with ourselves we all know what we'd love to do. We're too scared to admit it, or think we're too old, or that it's simply unfeasible for whatever reason. There are thousands and thousands of career options out there if we look hard enough. Take off your blinkers and look around you! You only have to look at your immediate circle of family and friends to see this.

Exercise

Without editing yourself, or holding back, answer the following questions.

- List five careers you wish you had.
- List five things you'd love to try if time or money were no object?

Exercise

I want you to pick three of the ideas you've listed above and spend the next month researching what you'd need to do in order to bring these new careers or jobs to fruition. Telephone the local colleges, universities or recruitment agencies. Speak to people you know who can help, go and see a careers' adviser or visit your local library. Gather all the information you need to make the right decision.

Your blueprint

When you have done this, look at each job or career in turn and see which has best fit with your values, passions and talents. It's important to point out that not all values and talents will be met through your work alone. For example, two of my values are love and security, and both are met from my home life (husband and children) and not from my job as a life coach. But, the key is the more a job fits with your values, passions and talents the happier you will be.

This is exactly what I did when I first discovered life-coaching. I knew nothing about the industry other than I thought it sounded fascinating. I had no idea what training was needed or how much it would cost me. And I had absolutely no idea how to start up and run a successful business. Yet here I am years later, running my own company. I've found a career that truly inspires me, combines all my interests, my skills, talents and values but, more importantly, I've found something I'm truly passionate about in life – helping others to achieve their full potential! Once you find a career in line with your blueprint, life has a way of just flowing; all of a sudden it feels like we're not fighting anymore and everything just falls into place.

Remember earlier? We're all looking for a fairy godmother to sort everything out for us. But life doesn't work this way. We have to instigate the magic, so don't be put off if your ideal career means retraining or learning new skills. If it's right for you, life will flow and become enjoyable in the process. There might be some temporary hard work but it's only transitory, it will soon pass. You can make as many excuses as you want, but the buck stops with you.

Sarah's story

Sarah worked as an office manager for a large advertising agency and had worked at the same company for over eight years. She was relied on for pretty much everything: from organising office supplies, planning the Christmas party to fixing the leaking toilet. She told me that she was totally bored; going to work had become a grinding chore and she needed a change, a new challenge to sink her teeth into. But, confessed Sarah, she had no idea what she wanted to do instead and her skills were fairly limited to admin-related roles.

We talked at length about Sarah's natural talents and passions, and made a long list of all the things she was good at and all the things she enjoyed doing in her spare time. At the top of her list was shopping. Sarah loved to shop and had a real eye for fashion. She instinctively knew what suited not only her body shape but also that of those around her. She even liked to alter items of clothing adding her own personal touch, by sewing on her own buttons or adding a funky belt. People always commented on her wonderful dress sense and how chic she looked. This gave Sarah a real sense of enjoyment and satisfaction. When we talked about fashion as one of her key natural talents Sarah just laughed out loud, 'If only I could make a career out of fashion!' She simply couldn't see what a gift she had. But I encouraged Sarah to move beyond her limiting thinking and look at each of her talents and passions with fresh eyes. We decided that some research was needed and she went away to list all the possible careers options available to her given her unique talents and passions. Shortly afterwards I received a call from a very lively and excited Sarah, who told me she'd had her epiphany. She had realised that she could put her eye for fashion to good use and make a career out of assisting others to shop for clothes and made them feel magnificent. Sarah had decided she wanted to open an image consultancy business where she could run workshops and personal consultations.

One month later Sarah enrolled on an image consultant course, which she planned to do alongside her current office manager role until such a time came where she was ready to open the doors to her own personal shopping consultancy.

Sarah's talent had always been there right in front of her nose, yet she'd failed to recognise it. Without Sarah's understanding of her talents and passions it would have been far more difficult for her to unveil the revelation that led her to make a career shift. We are all too quick to dismiss the obvious, but invariably all the good ideas are staring us plainly in the face. You might think your talents and passions are insignificant or limited to pastimes or hobbies, but it doesn't have to be this way. If you enjoy swimming perhaps you could become an instructor. If you enjoy gardening maybe you could become a landscape gardener. If you enjoy writing you could write a novel. Open your mind to the possibilities and the obvious will quickly become visible.

Chapter 6

Beyond your physical self

Let me now share with you a very personal experience I had a few years ago, which opened my eyes to a whole new way of living. This 'new way' has led me to become a life coach and inspired me to write this book.

Let me tell you about the day that changed my life forever.

It was a freezing cold bitter January afternoon. I had finished work and was driving to pick my daughter up from nursery. I pulled up outside, parking in my normal space by the railings, next to a large oak tree. I could see the sun setting in the distance and noticed two tiny robins in the tree hopping from branch to branch with no regard for my close proximity. I was 20 minutes early and under any other circumstances I would have gone straight into the nursery to collect my daughter, but I held back and took the opportunity to read a few pages of a book I had been given by a friend. This book had captivated me and I was tremendously excited by its content, as somewhere deep inside me I felt a resonance I hadn't felt before.

As I sat there with the car engine running and the windscreen slowly misting up, I turned the pages and found myself reading a meditation. In those days meditation was unfamiliar territory to me and my uneducated assumption of meditation was of rather unpleasant-smelling josh sticks, and old men sitting crossed-legged humming mantras. But, despite my limited understanding, I decided to take the opportunity to give it a go. I remember reading this little meditation two or three times, it was very simple; in fact, it was so simple I didn't quite see the point. Anyway, after making sure I had memorised the words, I inhaled a deeply and in my head repeated the words I had memorised. I don't think there are enough words in the English dictionary to describe what happen next.

As I sat in my car on that very normal January afternoon, something huge happened – not externally, but something happened inside me that was to change my world forever. As I effortlessly and with no expectation repeated the words of this short meditation in my head, all of a sudden an almighty gush of what I only describe as 'energy' entered my chest and moved up through the top half of my body and left out of the top of my head. This energy was unearthly, it was not something that I had experienced before and it was a more powerful feeling than anything I had felt in my entire life. This energy felt like total love, or euphoria, it was all-consuming and overwhelming. It's hard to say, but it probably only lasted 10 or 15 seconds. But in those few seconds my life changed. What the hell was it? My mind was racing and the tears were rolling down my face, I threw the book to the floor in shock. I couldn't make sense of the experience; there was no logical or rational explanation for it. It was very hard for me to take in as I've always been a realist. I like hard facts and figures to back things up – I've never been the airy-fairy type. The only thing I could think of was to call my grandmother who was a practising Christian. After spending 40 minutes on the telephone I felt calmer and composed myself enough to go into the nursery to collect my daughter (by this time I was almost an hour late).

In those remarkable few seconds I knew with all certainly that there was far more to life that I had been led to believe. I had discovered my inner spirit. My journey of awakening had begun! In those few moments I had moved beyond my physical body, beyond my mind and touched the world of spirit or pure energy, pure love and fulfilment itself. I had touched the 'real me'.

My comfortable reality had been turned upside-down and it took a few days before I felt 'with it', so to speak. My journey still continues, but I can tell you one thing, since that moment of realisation my life has flourished, grown, expanded and, for the first time, has far more meaning than I ever thought possible. It's important to point out that just because I had such a so-called 'spiritual' experience didn't mean from that point onwards my life was all rosy, but my life has made more sense and became far richer as a result.

I spent a long time trying to process and understand what happened to me that day. I read book after book, from religious books to books on quantum physics. I talked to mentors and spiritual gurus who could help me understand and simulate my experience. After a long search, I am happy to say I have come to a comfortable resting place. My conclusion is this: *beyond your physical body with all its imperfections and ailments, and far beyond your brain with its ineffective programming, who are you really?*

For me, the truth is simple: *We are spiritual (or energy) beings living in a physical reality. We are here as spiritual beings to play the game of life.*

We are conditioned to our material existence; we take life at face value and are accustomed to using only our five senses – sight, smell, touch, taste and hearing. Spirit is beyond all of these, it lies beneath the radar of our physical awareness and this is why so few people find it in their lifetime.

Spirit, or energy, is all there is and it's the 'real you' not the 'you' you have been fooled into believing you are. Spirit is pure fulfilment and love, and the more we connect with our inner spirit, the more fulfilling and satisfying our lives become.

Our bodies are our costume and our brains are our computer processor. But our brains, with their limiting beliefs, and our bodies, with their imperfections and illnesses, aren't what make us who we really are. The real you is pure positive energy – pure fulfilment itself!

Energy cannot die or be distinguished, it just changes form. Which, in turn, means that we never die we just change our form.

Our time on earth is not the end of the story, we are forever ongoing. We are here to enjoy our time on earth: to live, to play, to love, to experience all that this wonderful planet has to offer. Unfortunately, our lack of awareness means that our limited understanding covers and distorts this vital truth.

But here is the key. What I have come to learn is that the more we connect with our inner spirit the more pleasurable, smoother and gratifying our life becomes. The less we have to control, push, use force and manipulate things into being; spirit has the ability to do this for us, if we allow it.

This is a spiritual universe, from start to finish. This is the secret that we've all been missing. The more we can connect to our inner spirit the more harmonious our lives will become. Simple! There is a revolution afoot. People and science are starting to wake up to this truth.

When we really get a grasp of this, life is never really the same again. We must see through the mind's bravado to the truth. It is the collective mind (world beliefs) that has led us astray, and we just need to raise our consciousness to see through this illusion. Our inner spirit has the ability to re-program our minds for us, if we let it.

So what does all this mean? It means we are not limited, small, inadequate or restricted in any way as previously thought. We can be, do or have whatever we desire with help from our inner spirit. We just need to realise it and start believing! When we do our lives will change dramatically forever, and so will our entire human existence.

Once you learn how to connect to your inner spirit, people, circumstances, events, situations and opportunities will, seemingly, appear out of thin air to fulfil your very need. As if by magic! We can all connect with our inner power, we all have the ability to do this, but most of us don't know this extraordinary power exists right at our fingertips. It's waiting there for us to wake up so it can start helping us to manifest the life we deserve, a life full of bliss, harmony, peace, love and abundance.

In a moment I'm going to show you how to connect with your own inner spirit.

I have told you this story because I want you to open your mind to new possibilities, not so that you can try and recreate such an experience for yourself (spiritual awakening happens to everyone in different ways). I want you to expand your awareness beyond your physical existence. I urge you to seek your own answers. Do not take my word for it, or anyone else's for that matter. Your own truth lies with you, right now. To follow someone else's path is futile. The best strategy is to discover your own truth. Others may inspire, guide, give you direction, but ultimately you have to cut your own way through the jungle. Some people will tell you to head north, others will tell you to head south, and both will believe their way is right (and, of course, it is for them), but you alone have to find your true north or south.

Fear of the unknown

I know all this talk about energy or your inner spirit may be a little hard to digest, but no one's asking you to change your beliefs overnight. Self-discovery is an ongoing journey. In fact, does it ever end? Once we discover one thing, something else crops up and surprises us. But growth is our key to freedom. The more we learn, understand and experience the more free we become, and it's a wonderful phase. Take your time there is no rush!

Just remember, everyone feels fear on his or her journey to a better life. I've yet to meet the person who hasn't. Fear is a normal part of the growth process, whether it is fear about achieving a particular goal or fear of growing spiritually. Fear is a common part of everyday life and the sooner people realise this, the sooner they will stop running away and allow themselves to grow.

The joy of going within

After my profound experience in the car I decided that in order to find the answers I was looking for I needed to learn more about spirituality and my own inner spirit.

I decided that my first port of call would be meditation. I downloaded articles from the internet on how to meditate. I bought books and CDs and, eventually, after trying lots of different techniques I found my own style, my own way, which I still use to this day. How has it affected my life? Well the results have been profound. I've revealed a tranquillity that I'd never experienced before. I found an almighty support within that I didn't even know existed and I found clarity in my thinking which enabled me to see beyond all the limiting beliefs and behaviours that I'd been running since I was a child. In short, it changed my entire world and helped me to create the life I am living today.

I believe if more people were to understand the benefits of mediation and make it part of their daily routine we would live in a far more harmonious world. Modern life is manic; we have been fooled into living our lives using our minds as our confidant. But our minds are programmed with all sorts of limiting beliefs, which invariably create havoc in our lives. We need to bypass our minds as much as possible and connect directly with our inner spirit; that way our lives will be far more peaceful and enjoyable.

Most of us live our lives by the clock; we go to bed late, we get up before the sun has even risen and we pollute our bodies with unhealthy toxins. When we allow ourselves to 'go within', using mediation as a tool, time slows down, we clear our minds of negative clutter, we become less stressed and, more importantly, we feel happier. Plus it's free and accessible to everyone, yet we spend millions of pounds each year buying drugs that we think will make us feel more vibrant and indulging in material pleasures that we believe will bring us contentment. It's crazy, yet the solution is so simple.

I'd like to introduce you to three methods of going within and connecting with your own inner spirit. First, I want to show you how to meditate; second, I'd like to explain how positive visualisation can change your life for the better and help you to achieve your goals and, lastly, I'd like to talk to you about the power of prayer.

Meditation

There are numerous styles of mediating, such as breathing, candles, walking or mantras and there are lots of different schools of meditation, such as Buddhist, tantric and transcendental, to name but a few. You have to find what works for you. The technique below is my own personal method; it is what I find works best for me given my own schedule and lifestyle. But before I share my chosen method with you, I'd like you to consider the following tips.

- *Create your sanctuary.* Where is the best place for you to relax and where you're not likely to be disturbed? Perhaps the spare room, the garden, the dining room or even in the bath? Decide on the most suitable place and stick to the same location each time you meditate.

- *Use whatever you have to help you relax.* Consider lighting a candle while you meditate, or have a special ornament, photo or vase of flowers next to you. Anything that will help you to feel more at ease and relaxed.

- *Decide on your posture whilst meditating.* There are many different postures, from the most commonly known lotus position to the Egyptian, half-lotus, quarter-lotus and Japanese. You need to do a little research and see which one you prefer. I just lie down on my bed with my legs uncrossed and hands by my side, as I find this most relaxing.

- *Don't be disturbed.* Switch off the phone, lock the door and ensure you're not likely to be interrupted. You might meditate in the evenings when the kids are in bed and you know you're not going to be disturbed.

- *Write down any insights or thoughts.* Consider keeping a journal of your experiences or any insights you may have. When you become more proficient at meditating you'll start noticing you'll get more ideas during meditating or immediately afterwards.

- *Don't be scared.* If you feel anxious or uncomfortable for any reason whilst meditating remember you are not going anywhere so there is no need for fear. Meditating is not a form of 'medium-ship'. All you are doing is quietening your mind. You are going inwards in search of self-awareness. If you do begin to feel fearful just open your eyes slowly and bring your focus back to your surroundings.

- *Be guided by a voice.* Whilst learning to meditate you may find it useful to record your own voice to use as guided meditation, or perhaps you might like to consider buying a guided meditation CD to follow until you feel comfortable doing it on your own.

- *Commit.* You must find time to integrate this new routine into your daily schedule, just like brushing your teeth or taking a shower. If you're inconsistent, the results you receive will be inconsistent, so make a commitment to meditate as regularly as you can.

Start off with just five minutes' meditation a day, building up to 30 minutes or longer. Or, try small three-minute meditations throughout your day. Sometimes life may be very busy, but the more you meditate the more you'll start noticing the positive effects it has on you. You'll probably find your mind will be extremely active at first, reminding you of all the things you need to do, like doing the laundry, phoning your sister, making the kids' lunch for the next day, and so on. This is normal; you need to persist and eventually the nagging voices will gradually fade away and you'll be left with the most wonderful feeling of peace and bliss. And one wonderful day, when you're ready, you will have your own magical spiritual awakening.

Below I have outlined three simple meditations for you to try.

Relaxation

Take up your chosen position, close your eyes, relax and start noticing your breathing – breath in and out deeply until you feel relaxed. Bring your attention to your head and notice any tension you may be feeling in your forehead, eyes, cheeks, and so on, and release or let go of it. Once you have done this, bring your attention to your neck and shoulders; again, notice any tension you may be feeling and release or let go of it in the same way you did with your head. Slowly work through each body part in turn, from the top half of your body right through to your toes. Make sure you release any stress or tension as you go. By the time you reach your toes you should be feeling totally relaxed.

You may notice your Inner Critic popping up to remind you of all the things you need to do. It might point out that you have an itchy foot or a tickle in your throat, it might remind you that don't have time for this nonsense and tell get up and do something more useful. This is normal, even when you've been practising meditation for a long time. Recognise this voice and visualise shutting it outside the door, or imagine putting it in a box and locking it in there with a key. Sometimes it may take quite a while for this negative voice to dissipate, so be patient and give yourself time. Repetition is the key to mastering meditation.

Stay in this relaxed state for as long as you want. Enjoy the peace until you feel ready to come back to the room again.

Mantra

Take up your chosen position, close your eyes, relax, and start noticing your breathing – breath in and out deeply. Notice any repetitive thoughts and, as they pop into your head, release them in a way that works for you. Maybe imagine bursting them like you would a balloon; put your unwanted thoughts in a box or just imagine pressing the 'delete' key in your own head. Keep doing this until you feel your mind empty.

When you are ready repeat your chosen mantra, over and over again, slowly and concisely. Concentrate on the words as you say them. Here are some example mantras.

'Om' or 'Aum' is the most common and significant word of mantra tradition. It is considered as the root mantra of all mantras, but you can make up your own if you wish, try the following.

- I am love.
- I let go and I am free.
- I deserve only the best.
- I give and receive love.
- I release all anxiety and fear.
- I allow love to flow within me.

Stay in this relaxed state for as long as you want. Enjoy the peace until you feel ready to return to the room again.

White Light

Take up your chosen position and close your eyes, relax and start noticing your breathing – breath in and out deeply. Notice any repetitive thoughts and, as they pop into your head, release them in a way that works for you. As with the mantra above, burst them like you would a balloon, lock them in a box or press the 'delete' key in your head. Keep doing this until you feel your mind empty.

I want you to imagine in your mind's eye a large beam of bright pure white light cascading into the top of your head. Make the pure white light as bright as you possibly can. See the white light penetrating your head and clearing out any negative thoughts and beliefs that you hold. See the white light work its way through your entire body, washing away any unwanted energy as it does.

Once you have allowed this pure white light to penetrate your whole body, imagine it now forming a ball of light around your body, almost like a protective energy field that nothing can penetrate. Allow yourself to bask in this pure white light for as long as you need to.

Stay in this relaxed state for as long as you want to. Enjoy the peace until you feel ready to come back to the room again.

Exercise

Spend the next week trying out these three different techniques to see which one you prefer. Commit to mediating at least once a day for 30 days and see what a difference it makes.

Visualisation

Let me introduce you to the power of visualisation. I first stumbled upon visualisation early on in my journey and started using it immediately with remarkable results.

Visualisation is nothing new and has been taught by leading teachers and avatars for countless generations. Some of the world's most successful people use visualisation as part of their everyday life. Every successful person will tell you the same thing – they could see their success long before it actually happened!

Visualisation is one of the most effective ways of manifesting your dreams and goals. Whatever you picture in your mind, on some level, you are creating for yourself. The fact is that most of us unconsciously use this remarkable ability to imagine negative things happening to us instead of consciously focusing on what we actually *want* to happen.

Visualisation is the technique of using your conscious mind to make your subconscious mind aware of all of your dreams and desires. Everyone's mind works on two different levels; using visualisation will help you to get both parts of your mind working in synchrony. The conscious mind is the logical, 'thinking' mind that you are aware of and use every day. It is under your control and creates your thoughts. Your thoughts influence how you feel and what actions you take and the results that you get. Most of us focus our attention on the conscious mind when we are trying to achieve a particular goal. We make plans we try to think positively, but somehow we still fail. Using just the conscious mind alone will get you nowhere fast. The secret to getting results is to use the subconscious mind as well!

All of our emotions, experiences and beliefs are nicely tucked away in our subconscious mind, and we are completely unaware of most of them. This is the 'feeling part of the mind and it influences our conscious thoughts and behaviours. Simply put, your subconscious mind is where all your 'programming' takes place. Visualisation helps you to tap into your subconscious and change the old programming that is stopping your goals, dreams or desires coming to fruition. So when you have both parts of your mind working in together you will achieve success much more easily.

Many experiments have been carried out into the power of positive visualisation. Scientists have linked an Olympic sprinter up to biofeedback equipment so they could monitor his brain activity. They then asked the athlete to sprint around a track as if he were running an actual race and then asked him to run the same race in his head, while sitting in a chair linked to the same biofeedback equipment. Amazingly, the scientists found that the same brain activity was generated when the athlete ran the race and when he ran it in his head. So what does this tell us? That the sprinter's brain couldn't tell the difference between running the race physically or in his mind – to his brain the power of imagination is as real as running the race.

What most of us don't realise is that all creation (including our own lives) starts from within our own mind and inner spirit. We are so misled that we believe we must change the outer circumstances in our lives: people, places and situations, when in fact we need first to go within.

When you are visualising you are changing the programming of your mind. You are changing unwanted thoughts, beliefs, habits and behaviours, and are 're-wiring' your brain! Remember, you are just a mass of electrical circuits, but if you have some faulty wiring you can change it by using mental imagines and pictures. The reason why visualisation is so successful is because when you practise it, you are creating vivid pictures in your mind's eye of yourself with what it is you desire, whether that be better health, a more loving relationship, a new car, a better job or more money. You generate new positive thoughts, feelings and beliefs that help re-program your mind, but you also invoke the power of spirit or the Law of Attraction to help you manifest what it is you're wanting. And that's when miracles start happening! All success starts from within. Like Thomas Eddison and the light bulb or Alexandra Graham Bell with the telephone, they saw their success in their mind long before they actually succeeded.

Remember, visualisation is the field where everything is created!

Let me demonstrate. I want you to close your eyes (once you've read this, of course!) and imagine you're holding a juicy ripe lemon in your hand.

The lemon is a vibrant yellow and its skin is bumpy to the touch. It has just come out of the fridge and feels cold in the palm of your hand. Even though the fruit has not been cut you can smell it. Imagine picking up a knife and slicing the lemon in half on a kitchen work surface. As you do this citrus juices spurt out and some of the juice runs on to your finger. You put both the knife and the lemon down and quickly lick the juice off your hand. It's terribly sour!

Is your mouth watering yet?

What this little exercise demonstrates is that using the power of your imagination you can stimulate your saliva glands without even tasting the fruit for real. So if your imagination can do this, what else it is capable of generating?

The first thing I noticed when I first started visualising was how enjoyable it was, like a wonderful daydream that I rarely wanted to end. It was really pleasurable, mainly because I was in control of the images I created in my head and, of course, because I was in control I ensured that all the movies I would play out were positive, fun and exhilarating, where only good things happen to me.

When I first started visualising I was in a job that I didn't particularly enjoy. I never seemed to have enough time, my savings were minimal and I didn't feel as if I was being the best mother I could be. There was plenty of room for improvement in my life at that time and I had lots of ideas of how I would have wanted my life to look instead.

At that time I'd arrive home at 6 pm each night. I would quickly bathe my daughter, feed her dinner and tuck her up safely in bed. I would then rummage through the freezer to find something I could cook for my partner and myself with the least amount of effort possible. My life was hectic, and deep down I was desperate for change. Even though it would have been easier to just flop on to the settee with a huge glass of wine, I would summon up the energy to spend 10 minutes meditating followed by a further 15 minutes of visualising – every evening without fail. I would visualise myself doing a job I thoroughly enjoyed (even though I had no idea what that job was). I would see myself sitting in my home office, which hadn't even been built, working away on a computer I hadn't even bought yet. I would observe myself typing away, no idea what I was writing, but I would feel a sense of satisfaction and fulfilment from the work I was doing. I would visualise checking my bank account and smiling as I looked at a healthy balance. It felt wonderful. I'd look around at my happy home with lots of space and beautiful new furniture. I'd see all the DIY completed and notice how all my cupboards were neatly displayed with everything in place. I would look outside and see my fine-looking vegetable garden lush with fresh green salads and herbs, and I would see my daughter playing barefoot on the daisy-laden grass. I would see myself having time to peruse my many cookbooks and prepare nutritious meals for my family. I saw myself having regular dinner parties and playing the perfect hostess. I pictured myself having time to enjoy my daughter to the full, bathing her, playing with her and reading her endless stories. Bliss! I saw my life exactly how I wanted it to be. And I did this consistently every night, month after month after month, even when there was no inkling of change on the horizon.

Things didn't really start changing until almost six months into this process. To see results takes time and all depends on how much you're willing to commit. The more you put in, the more you get out. I started to notice changes happening: opportunities and ideas came into my awareness, along with new people, new possibilities and new information. I wish I could say that one day I woke up with my fairy godmother at my side and I was living my dream life, but it wasn't quite that simple. Where would be the fun in that! I had to get off my backside and take opportunities as they presented themselves to me. Slowly but surely things started to alter. The changes didn't always happen in the way I expected, but my life did start to expand.

It wasn't until almost two years later, on a beautiful summer afternoon, when I was sitting in my new dining room (recently built) writing an article for a magazine that I suddenly became aware of the journey I had taken. There I was; I had given up my marketing job and had set up my own business as a life coach. I had more time to spend with my family and do the things I truly enjoyed. And I had even planted my own vegetable patch! It was a moment I will never forget. In those few seconds I realised my power. I had created the life I was living, no one else but me! I had created it not by trying to force things to change, but by going within. The more I committed to my inner world the more joy I experienced in my outer world. It was that simple!

The most common thing I encounter when teaching people about visualisation is that most people don't believe in their own imagination. These days we tend to use our intellect far more than our imagination or intuition. We think too much, we try to be logical and rationalise everything until we can make sense of it. Everything that remains unexplained is simply dismissed because it cannot be proven. But, as mentioned before, science is starting to uncover some new truths about the human mind and spirit. Our imagination is the medium through which we focus our mental energy to create our own happiness or hardship in this world. Once we grasp this, our lives will really start to transform.

The great thing with visualisation is that you can be your own scientist. Try it and see for yourself. My only disclaimer is this; first, you must be clear about your desired outcome (your goals) and, second, you must commit for a set period of time. There is no point trying once, twice or even five times, because it's simply not enough. Commit for five minutes a day for three months. Let's face it, five minutes a day just before you go to sleep is hardly asking too much. Is it?

Tips when using visualisation

- *Practice.* Repetition is the key to any new skill.
- *See yourself in the third person*, as if you were watching a film and you are the lead actor or as if you are looking at yourself.
- *Put emotions into your dream.* Feel how it would feel to have achieved your goals.
- *Make it real.* Visualise colour, imagine smells; make the scene as real as possible.
- *Keep it positive.* Do not let negative thoughts or feelings in whilst visualising.

Below I have outlined four different visualisations for you to try.

Seeing into your future

This is the exercise I used to manifest the changes in my life. Try it, but remember, to see the effects you must commit to practising it every day.

Find somewhere you can relax, perhaps sitting in your favourite chair or lying on the bed. Make yourself comfortable and start breathing in and out deeply until you feel your body relax. When you're ready close your eyes.

Once you are ready I want you to imagine how you want your life to be, approximately one year into the future.

Focus as much as you can on the detail, using sound, colour, touch and taste in your daydream. Make the picture bright, vivid and as real as possible. Notice how you look, what are you wearing? Notice your surroundings, what are they like? Where are you? What is the weather like today? Who are you sharing your day with? How will you be spending your evening? What are you doing for a living and what is it you enjoy most about your work? How do you feel about you financial situation now?

Spend some time looking back at the last year: what are you most proud of achieving? What is it you now believe about yourself? How do you feel about this?

Once you're happy you've spend enough time living in your future, slowly bring your attention back to your surroundings. Smile and know your desired future is yours for the taking.

Self-healing

Whether you're as healthy as an ox or you're currently feeling unwell, visualisation has been proved to be extremely powerful at aiding recovery, from a common cold to more serious illnesses. Try the following.

As before, find somewhere you can relax. Make yourself comfortable and start breathing in and out deeply until you feel your body relax. When you're ready close your eyes.

Imagine your immune system in a way that resonates with you: perhaps you see lots of bulldozers driving around your body; maybe you find it easier to visualise a triumphant army marching through your system or maybe you see lots of tiny little fish swimming through your bloodstream. It doesn't really matter what you choose.

Now, imagine your illness (whatever that may be) as a dark grey area within your body, notice its size and location. Visualise your chosen immune system and see it saturate the dark grey area; see this area reducing in size – becoming smaller and smaller until you cannot see it anymore.

Once you have done this mentally thank your immune system for its sterling job and send it back on its way to patrol your body, protecting it from further invasion.

Finally, I want you to now see and feel your body as healed and healthy. When you're ready, slowly bring your attention back to your surroundings. Smile and know that your body is completely healthy. Feel the difference!

The real you

This exercise is good at increasing confidence and self-esteem, and is a great way to start your day.

Find somewhere you can relax and make yourself comfortable. Start breathing deeply in and out until you feel your body relax. When you're ready close your eyes.

Imagine another 'you' standing in front of you. This is your 'perfect' you.

Look at your body and admire all things you like: look at your hair and skin, and notice how healthy they look. This is your true self and the most wonderful version of 'you' that can imagine.

Now notice how your true self stands, talks, moves; notice the confidence that oozes out of your body. Notice how relaxed and comfortable your other self is. Your true self has achieved everything you have ever wanted or dreamed of.

I want you to now to imagine stepping into your true self's body. So your two bodies have now become one. Notice the difference in how you feel. Look through the eyes of your true self, what do you see? How are things different?

Now let your mind wonder and imagine all the things you would do if you were living in your true self's body all the time. What differences would occur? What would you spend your time doing? How would you feel?

When you feel this new confidence flowing through your body slowly bring your attention back to your surroundings.

Create your ideal day in advance

This exercise is a good way to start each and every day. Try it for a week and see what happens.

Find somewhere you can relax. Make yourself comfortable, and start breathing in and out deeply until you feel your body relax. When you're ready close your eyes.

Mentally take note of all the wonderful things you already have in your life – from your home, friends, family, your health or perhaps your material possessions. Note everything you have to be grateful for, big or small. Leave nothing out!

As before, I want you to imagine another 'you' standing in front of you. This is your 'perfect' you. Look at your body and admire all things you like. Look at your hair and skin, and notice how healthy they look. This is your true self and the most wonderful version of 'you' that can imagine.

Imagine stepping into your true self's body so your two bodies now become one. Notice the difference it makes to your confidence and the way that you feel. Imagine carrying out your day living in the body of your true self.

Today you are going to be the real you! See yourself carrying out all your normal activities and talking to your family, friends and colleagues. See how wonderful your day is and how smoothly it runs.

Notice how self-assured you are and how happy you feel. Take a couple of minutes to plan your day, exactly how you want it to go.

When you're ready, slowly bring your attention back to your surroundings. Have a wonderful day!

Exercise
Spend the next week trying out these four different visualisations to see which one you prefer. Commit to visualising at least once a day for 30 days and see what difference it makes.

The power of prayer

Although I don't follow a particular religion, I am a huge advocate of the power of prayer. I grew up with religious roots, mainly from my mother's upbringing as a catholic and whilst we rarely went to church other than at Christmas and Easter time, I was brought up always to say my prayers every night before going to bed. For me, praying wasn't so much as a religious ritual but more an ingrained habit or obligation. In a way it was like brushing my teeth or taking a shower. It wasn't until I jumped on to my spiritual path that I truly understood its true meaning and power.

Prayer, like meditation and visualisation, is just another method of going within and connecting to your inner spirit.

There have been many studies into power of prayer and meditation, and recent work has shown that people who either pray, or are prayed for, recover far quicker from illness than those who are not (see http://news.bbc.co.uk/1/hi/health/485268.stm).

For me prayer is just a direct connection to spirit, to your true self. When you connect with this part of yourself you are using the power of your all-fulfilling spirit to create the life you were always meant to live until your mental programming took hold of you. I find it a wonderful support, almost like I have a best friend to share my life with: *someone who is always there and is never judgemental or critical*. It is my belief that through mediation, visualisation and prayer we are connecting with our inner spirit, and when we do this we transcend all material baggage and negative beliefs, habits and behaviours. Connecting regularly with our spirit will help us to re-program our minds; all we have to do is make a commitment to 'hook up' as much as possible through whichever means works for us.

How do you pray? Well, however you want to. There are no hard and fast rules. When I pray it's just like I'm having a friendly conversation with my Inner Guide. I tell my Inner Guide about all my concerns and worries, and ask for new insights and ideas to present themselves to me. It's just like talking to an old friend. Pray to whom or whatever feels comfortable – perhaps God, to your Inner Guide or maybe a relative. If it feels right to you, you cannot go wrong.

Connecting mind, body and spirit

What I have come to realise is that we are all made up of three different levels. The body, which is made up of all our skin, muscles, organs, blood, bones, cells and so on. Our mind, which is made up of billions of neuro-pathways and circuits, where all our programming is stored just like a computer hard drive. And our spirit, part of us that is eternal pure energy. Science has spent the last 200 years or so investigating the body. We understand more now than we have ever done about human anatomy. Science has also made huge advances during the last 30 years or so in studying the power of the mind and the way our brains operate. Our spirit, on the other hand, is yet to be understood fully by the scientific community. Things such as the Law of Attraction, the afterlife and God are still mysteries and are often dispelled because of a lack of evidence to support them.

Science is uncovering truths about the human race that will turn our current reality on its head. But remember, just because you don't understand something, doesn't mean it's not true. It's all part of evolution: *truth changes!* The Victorians would have been amazed by the concept of mobile phones, aircraft or the world wide web. Look how much has changed! Look how technology has advanced. Science has reached a turning point. We have locked ourselves in our current paradigm and haven't even considered that there might be a better way. Truth changes and so does scientific fact.

How can a fish know it is in water? To a fish no other reality is imaginable!

When we live our lives using only body and mind alone we find ourselves struggling. Our bodies let us down, and life seems to be inconsistent and complicated. We've been misled. We've all been missing a crucial part of the jigsaw! We are so much more than our bodies and minds, we are also spiritual beings. When we can start nurturing the spiritual side of ourselves our life becomes a joy to live. How? I'm not quite sure, but when you combine all three aspects of yourself, mind, body and spirit, miracles start to unfold in your life.

As we continue through the remainder of this book I want you to make a commitment to start nurturing your inner spirit in a way that feels right for you. If you do you will find that your journey to living a wonderful life will be smoother, easier and more enjoyable. Achieving your goals will become effortless. Don't get me wrong, there are lots of people who are hugely successful utilising their body and mind alone to achieve their endeavours, but what I'm saying is by adding a third missing element (your spirit) your journey will blessed in every way possible. Instead of fighting your way through the jungle single-handed, you will receive an unearthly support that only spirit can provide. Things will fall into place with minimal amount of effort. Circumstances will present themselves at the perfect time and the right people will come into your life just when you need them most. Isn't this the way it's supposed to be? Why would you want to struggle when you don't have to!

When life gets tough or complicated it's a huge warning sign to ourselves that we've lost our connection with spirit. When things start going in the wrong direction it's time to stop and go within. If you can stay connected regularly you will lead an enchanted life. You will become one of those people where others say, 'What it is she does that's different to me?'

How do you stay connected? Through determination and commitment: you cannot expect to go to the gym for a month and have the perfect physique for the rest of your life, that's just crazy! The more you connect with your inner spirit the more joy and pleasure you will receive in your day-to-day life. You need to create a daily routine or ritual of going within, via whatever method works best for you. Maybe that's mediation, perhaps spending lots of time in nature, with animals, or maybe visualisation or prayer. Find a method of connection that works for you. You will know what feels right.

Exercise

Over the next month make sure you connect with your spirit on a daily basis, even five minutes a day will do. The more you connect the better results you will get.

Simon's story

Simon came to me as quite a sceptic when it came to anything 'spiritual' or 'non-scientific'. He was what he called 'a realist'. Naturally I was slightly hesitant about introducing meditation, visualisation and the like, but knowing just how powerful and life-changing these practices had been in my life, I felt almost duty-bound to present them to Simon and let him make up his own mind.

Although he was dubious, Simon listened to my reasoning and was more open-minded than he'd led me to believe. He had been quite ill suffering with a long-term condition for years; he'd had endless drugs from the medical profession in attempts to 'fix' the problem, to no avail. So he decided he had nothing to lose and would try meditation as a way of controlling and, he hoped, reducing his symptoms. Simon went out and bought a book on mediation and started trying lots of different techniques and styles until he found one that he felt comfortable with.

He told me that he had great difficulty trying to quieten his mind of all its daily clutter and would repeatedly end up feeling frustrated and irritated. We decided that Simon needed to find a suitable way of clearing his mind of all its unnecessary ramblings prior to meditation. We talked at length and came up with lots of different techniques that might help until he found something that he felt would work for him. He decided that when a thought popped into his head he could simply press the imaginary 'delete' button just as he would on his computer keyboard and any unwanted thoughts would simply disappear from his consciousness. This was a breakthrough as this method enabled him to clear his mind with ease, making meditation much more enjoyable. Simon committed to meditating three times a week initially, and the results were quite amazing. After just one month he found that not only was he less stressed at work, he was more content at home and his physical symptoms had subsided considerably. He was flabbergasted that something so simple could make such a difference to his life. Simon subsequently joined a local meditation class and made sure he found time to meditate every night. The more he saw the benefits the more he found time to incorporate this new practice into his life.

Over a period of six months the changes in Simon's life were profound. Not only did he feel happier, more vibrant and more satisfied with life, he also felt and looked healthier than he had in years. People were commenting on how look well he looked, asking what his secret was!

The great thing with meditation or visualisation is that you don't have to take anyone's word for it. Try them out for yourself and be your own scientist. My only caveat is that you must commit unequivocally for set period of time. Nothing changes overnight. Meditating once, twice, three times isn't enough to make a difference, it need to be practised regularly over considerable time for the results to be seen in your everyday life. But if you do this you'll be amazed at what manifests!

Chapter 7

Making it happen

Congratulations! You're almost there and have arrived at the final two chapters of the book. Let's review your journey so far. In the first few chapters we took time to explore what was currently going on in your life, and looked at all the potential areas for change. I then encouraged you to expand your comfort zone and start thinking about setting some big, juicy life-changing goals. Chapters 3 and 4 took you on an inward journey into the workings of your mind, and we crept inside dark crevasses of your psyche looking for all the outdated programming and how it is affecting or will continue to affect your life if you don't do something about it. And, more importantly, I shared with you my best tips and techniques which you'll need to adopt a fresh new attitude; these will not only help you achieve wonderful things they will also assist you in making your comfort zone far wider than ever before. Finally, I took you on a spiritual journey into the realms of 'energy', and we looked at the Law of Attraction, at mediation and visualisation.

You've done all the required work beneath the surface and I think it's about time you got into action! Let's face it, if you really want to make some big changes to your life, you're going to have to get out there and start making it happen. And that's exactly what we are going to do now. And, yes, it means you *are* going to have to do something!

In this chapter I'm going to show you the nitty-gritty of how to transfer your goals from paper to reality. I'm going to show you everything you need to know to make sure you reach your desired target, whether that is to secure a promotion, to change careers completely, to start your own business, meet someone special, reach spiritual enlightenment, get fit or become financially free. Whatever your goal, the process is the same.

It's time to dig out the three goals you set yourself way back in Chapter 2. But, before you go any further, and it's been a while since you set your goals, I want you to ask yourself the following questions again.

- Are these really my goals?
- Am I committed to achieving these goals?
- Do these goals excite me?
- Will achieving these goals make me feel happy?

It's vitally important that you set the right goals, because if you don't you're setting yourself up to fail. How do you know if you've set the right goals?

- You feel extremely excited and scared at the same time.
- You can't seem to focus on anything because you are too busy daydreaming.
- You feel impatient and immediately start researching your goals.
- You wake up in the morning and for the first time in years you have a smile on your face.
- You phone your mum, sister, brother or friends to share your overwhelming excitement.

If you're still unsure about whether you've set the right goals, go back and read Chapter 2 again, or, alternatively, get someone to give you a hand.

Taking responsibility

I hope you are starting to realise that *no one but you* is responsible for your life. It really is time to grow up and stop blaming your parents, your job, your partner or the state of the economy for the way your life is. It's time to stand on your own two feet and start building the life you deserve because, believe me, if you don't do it no one else will! Every successful person knows this truth. If you think writing your goals down is enough to make them manifest you're deluding yourself. There is no fairy godmother out there to magically wave her wand and make your dreams all come true before your eyes. If, secretly, this is what you're waiting for you're going to be waiting for a long time. Remember, *you're your fairy godmother*! There is nothing worse than living with regret. I'd hate to be 80 years old and wish I had written a book, started a business, run a marathon for charity, manufactured that product, met the right partner, had children, lost weight or whatever. Living with regret is excruciating and fills us with profound disappointment.

No more excuses, no more procrastinating. Your future is in your hands!

I often meet people whom, when I ask: 'What do you want to do with the rest of your life?' tell me about their dreams and ambitions, but as soon as the words leave their mouths they bombard me with copious reasons as to why it won't – or can't – happen. They tell me, 'I've love to retrain as a teacher, but I'm too much in debt' or 'I'd love to open my own café but I'm not clever enough and wouldn't have a clue where to start.' These are all excuses. I remember when I decided to retrain and become a life coach; I was so excited I could hardly contain my enthusiasm. I knew I would have to retrain and I knew it would cost me money, but I wasn't prepared for the shock I received when I found out just how much my training would cost. How on earth was I going to afford it? I had a little money saved in the bank, but nowhere near enough. My Inner Critic revelled in the news and flooded my mind with thoughts like 'Oh well, it was a nice idea' and 'You wouldn't have succeeded anyway'. The next morning I awoke with two choices: either I forgot the whole thing or I would throw caution to the winds and follow my dream, whatever the cost. I made my choice and thank goodness I did. It wasn't easy, but it has been life-changing. It was the best decision I ever made. Sometimes we just have to take a risk. How easy it would have been for me to remain within my comfort zone and continue to let the Inner Critic rule my life. Yes, very easy. But if I hadn't made the decision to start afresh I would probably still be where I was at five years ago, and that thought just fills me with dread.

Start believing your goals are possible

Let's get clear about something. If you are going to achieve your goals you're going to need to start believing they are feasible. If you have any doubts whatsoever you are simply going to slow yourself down or, worse still, you will set yourself up to fail. It's essential that you implement the right beliefs to ensure your victory. If you put your mind to it you can change anything in your life: your job; your relationship; your health; your home; your financial status; your stress level. But you must start believing it's possible.

In order to make a start let's recapitulate on the previous chapters and start employing the techniques I've covered so far.

- Create new affirmations for each goal you have set and start repeating them to yourself on a daily basis.
- Create a 'vision board' containing all the images and photographs you can find which represent the life you are aspiring to.
- Research others who have successfully walked the path before you, and read inspiring autobiographies or other 'self-help' or spiritual books.
- Tune into your Inner Guide as much as you can and listen for the messages that are given to you.
- Meditate daily and ensure you regularly visualise your future exactly as you want it, by using the examples in Chapter 6.
- Most importantly, as you start moving towards your goals, begin creating your list of evidence, as this will be undeniable proof that your beliefs are starting to change.

If you do all of these things your beliefs will, without doubt, start to alter.

When I started my voyage to becoming a life coach, like most of us, my self-belief was limited. I had lots of doubts and fears, which only began to alter when I started practising the techniques listed above. On my car journey to work I would switch off the radio and use the 20-minute drive to repeat my affirmations over and over again, and on the way home I would listen to inspirational audiotapes from well-known authors from around the world. At work I would often nip off to the ladies and take time for two- or three-minute 'mini-mediations'. When I arrived home I would then find the time to meditate and visualise my life as I wanted it. I spent every spare moment with my nose in self-help books and would read one book every week, adopting any new methods that I thought were useful.

My commitment and determination were irrefutable. I completely saturated myself in anything and everything that I could find which would help me to create the right mind-set and, ultimately, help me to achieve my goals.

Exercise
Ask yourself: 'What are the three things I am going to do from now on that will help me to start believing my goals are possible?'

Getting out of your comfort zone

A prerequisite to achieving your goals is leaving your comfort zone, and that is going to feel uncomfortable. Most of us live our lives nicely 'tucked in' within our self-created comfort zones. Although a nice, quiet, uneventful life without turbulence or unrest sounds lovely, it's unlikely to happen. We all have to face changes throughout our lives, whether we like it or not. We have two choices: either instigate the change or wait for it to be forced upon us. I know which one I'd rather choose. Life isn't about avoiding change at all costs, or about wrapping yourself up in cotton wool; this is no way to exist and you'll end up growing old with many disappointments and regrets.

In order to grow and expand we need to experience new things, and when we do new opportunities arise, new people walk into our lives and fresh doors open up for us to walk through. I believe that each one us is programmed to look for ways of enriching or upgrading who we are. Deep down we all want more, we all want to feel satisfied and we all want to be happy. But to do so we need to leave the familiar boundaries of our comfort zone. And, do you know what: it's never as bad as you imagine it's going to be! We'll talk more about facing your fears in the final chapter.

Exercise

List five things you can do this week that will push you to expand your comfort zone – from driving a new route to work or buying clothing in a colour you wouldn't normally wear to making that phone call you've been putting off for weeks. I promise you'll feel fantastic with your achievements.

Who sets goals?

Most people think goals are actually glorified New Year's resolutions. And, for most of us, this is true. It has been said that only 3% of the population set goals for themselves, and those who do are among the wealthiest in the country.

How many of us have made a New Year resolution on 1 January, either to stop smoking, stop eating chocolate, stop drinking, get out of debt, find love, or whatever, only to find out that by 20 January you've forgotten all about it? We may all identify with this on some level.

Most of us drift haphazardly from one year to the next, never really stopping to see whether we're travelling the right direction. Try this analogy: when we go into a restaurant we have a look at the menu and within a few minutes we decide what we fancy. The waiter takes our order and we relax, knowing full well that our food is on its way. But, what if we went into the restaurant and stated that we were hungry but couldn't decide what to order? How could the waiter bring you your food – you would remain hungry! It's the same with life: we remain unfulfilled if we don't decide what we want.

It's easy to see the absurdity of the behaviour in the analogy, yet most of us act like this when dealing with our lives. If you want to steer your life in the right direction you've to grab hold of the menu and start deciding what you want because if you don't you'll either remain hungry or someone else will order for you and you won't like what you get.

It has been proved that those who set goals achieve far greater things than those who don't. When you think about it, it makes complete sense. When you have a target in front of you, you become incredibility focused and determined. Think about a time in your life when this was true for you? Achieving your targets or goals feels truly amazing. It's like a drug that keeps you moving forwards from one goal to the next. As soon as you reach one goal you are looking for the next challenge, your next 'achievement fix'. And through this process your self-belief increases and your confidence soars. This is why some of the successful individuals in the world, such as Donald Trump, Alan Sugar, Bill Gates or Madonna for example, continue to achieve. They didn't make their first goal and then decide that was it; they used the momentum of achievement to carry them forwards to lead outstanding lives. Once you start goal-setting you, too, will find this is true.

Why people don't achieve their goals

There are a few crucial mistakes that people make when setting goals. First, people set too small a goal. A client came to see me insisting that one of her key goals was to book a summer holiday to Greece, even though she went abroad every year. Now this is all very well, but when I asked the client if the holiday would happen anyway, regardless of her working with me or not, she stuttered and agreed it would. She didn't need a life coach to help her book a holiday that was going to happen away. Remember, your goals must be big enough to take you out of your comfort zone. When I probed a little further it turned out that the client had always wanted to run in the London Marathon in aid of the charity Breast Cancer Awareness. Now there's a more challenging goal if ever I heard one! Goals must be big enough to excite you but fill you with fear at the same time – that's when you know your comfort zone is being stretched. Setting too small a goal might well be comfortable, but it's just a cop-out! You're fooling yourself.

Conversely, people also tend to set themselves goals that are too big. Goals so gigantic that even the world's most successful individual might struggle to achieve them. They set themselves up to fail right from the start. Yes, your goals must stretch you, but they must also be realistic. If someone came to me wanting to earn a million pounds within one month I would have to ask whether this goal was really achievable and, if so, on what basis. There is absolutely nothing wrong with setting yourself a big goal like this, but I would suggest breaking it down into manageable chunks and setting a pragmatic deadline. Remember, your goals should be attainable within a six-month period. If you're unsure whether your goal is too big or too small, re-read Chapter 2 for clarification.

People also tend to overlook the need to break their goals down into manageable, bite-sized pieces, leaving them feeling completely confused and overwhelmed. One of the most important things you do when working with a life coach is to analyse your goals and then break them down into smaller portions and deal with each portion at a time. This way you don't allow yourself to become weighed down or besieged.

Other major pitfall is not doing the internal work required, such as getting the right mind-set or attitude. As mentioned before, if you are harbouring negative beliefs towards your goal, no matter how hard you try to push and force things to happen, you will remain in the same loop. Remember, *what you believe becomes your reality*. If you believe your goals are unachievable they will be. This is why it is important not to set too big a goal. If you want to achieve your goals you must do the internal work as well.

Finally, people set themselves up to fail by telling too many people about their dreams and ambitions. I know when you get an incredible idea the first thing you want to do is share it with those you love – it's only natural. But, as much as people care about us they can pour icy cold water over our ideas. I call them 'dream-stealers'. Why? Well, it's not because they don't love us or that they think our idea is rubbish; it's because it highlights their own imperfections or lack of drive to live the life they want for themselves. In short, people feel bad if you're taking control of *your* life and they're not in charge of theirs. I have clients come to me, having set wonderful, life-changing goals in their initial session, only to find that they come back the following week wanting to downsize their ideas. When I ask why, it's invariably because they've talked it through with their partner, friends, mum or brother, who, in turn, has led the client to believe that maybe their goal is a bit too farfetched or unrealistic. This subsequently influences the mind-set of the client and their ability to believe in themselves. Do not let other people smother your dreams. Keep your light under a bushel. Be selective about whom you share you dream and ideas with. We'll talk about this further in a moment.

How to make it happen

There are six primary elements to accomplishing your goals:

- Break your goals down into strategies.
- Take consistent weekly action.
- Create a support network.
- Become accountable.
- Keep the excitement alive.
- Don't tell the world.

Let's look at each in turn.

Break your goals down into strategies

Once you have established your goals you need to take each one in turn and divide it into smaller chunks. I call these chunks 'strategies' or 'milestones'. By doing this you don't become overwhelmed by the magnitude of the journey you're about to embark on. Once we allow ourselves to become overwhelmed we start procrastinating and postponing our actions. This invariably means that our goals never even make it off the ground. Look at it like this. If I said to you 'I want to drive from London to Madrid in one day, in one continuous journey without stopping or slowing' would it be realistic? Of course not: but if I was to say 'I want to drive from London to Madrid over three days, and stop off in Paris, Bordeaux and Zaragoza before finally reaching Madrid on the third day' how realistic is this? You cannot expect to complete your journey overnight. It takes time. And if you want to be successful you must break your goal down into milestones. For example, running a marathon may well seem impossible until you have broken it down into manageable chunks of, first, running 3 miles, then 7, then 12, then 18 before finally moving to the full 26. During this process you're building strength and stamina (both physically and mentally), which will guarantee your personal victory. Without strategies you simply won't know where to start. Having a clear plan of action will put you on the most efficient path to achieving your goals. When we don't set a clear plan of action we jump ahead of ourselves, causing ourselves more work in the long term.

Setting your strategies is straightforward, but it might be worth getting someone to help you, as no doubt they'll think of things you won't. Sit down with a blank piece of paper and brainstorm all the major areas you think you'll need to cover in order to reach each of your goals. Don't worry about the order at this stage; just list everything that comes to mind. Remember, you're not listing physical actions (that will come later); you're putting together an inventory of the main areas you're going to need to cover on your journey. I suggest setting between three and eight strategies for each of your goals. If you find you have a list of nine or more, refine and amalgamate your list until you have no more than eight. Say you were planning your wedding day, for instance. As I'm sure you can imagine, there are a million and one things to do before the big day arrives. So rather than getting yourself bogged down you would create a series of milestones to cover, one at a time, putting them into the order in which they'll need to be tackled. For example, your strategy list might include: the venue, catering, theme, outfits, guest list, transport and honeymoon. This breaks the whole goal down into manageable bite-sized pieces and it becomes less of a monster to tackle. You then concentrate on each strategy at a time. You do not move onto your next strategy until you've finished working on your current one. This way you're taking smaller steps towards your goal, rather than going round in circles. Remember, *you eat an elephant one mouthful at a time*!

Here are three examples of goals and how your strategies might look.

Goal: To go on a once-in-a-lifetime holiday around the world

- Establish resources.
- Decide on the locations.
- Look at finances.
- Devise a timetable.
- Book holiday.
- Prepare for leaving.

Goal: To increase my self-esteem so I can meet someone special by Christmas

- Look at beliefs and behaviours.
- Research new techniques to change mind-set.
- Adopt techniques.
- Change mind-set.
- Look at ways of meeting new people and expanding social network.

Goal: To find a career that turns me on by March

- Establish likes and dislikes of current career.
- Look at values.
- Define natural abilities and talents.
- Look at all career options.
- Decide on three career paths to research.
- Decide on one path to peruse.
- Start training.

Take consistent action

Once you've created your strategies it's time to get into action. This is the point where you need to get off the sofa, go out there and start bringing your goals alive.

You could plan and strategise until the cows come home but this won't change your life a jot. Actions are the key to success! They are the engine to your dreams. You set actions by taking each strategy in turn and creating a series of small steps. I would recommend setting three or four actions every day, from making a phone call or arranging a meeting to carrying out research. If you were to take three or four actions every day that's 20 actions per week, which takes you 20 steps closer to your goal. If you keep this momentum up you'll achieve your goals in record time. Keep your strategies to hand when planning your actions, as they are your overall road map leading you to your desired destination; remember only to set actions around your current strategy – tempting as may be, don't jump ahead!

Perhaps you could sit down every Sunday night and write a 'To do' list of all the actions you intend to take in the week ahead. Sunday night might be 'planning' night. It ensures that every Monday morning you wake up full of enthusiasm and passion. Never, ever, feel directionless when you have a 'To do' list to work through. And the best thing is having the satisfaction of crossing off items as you do them! Get into the habit of doing this and you're on the road to victory.

There is one final ingredient to setting actions: remember to follow the signs the universe provides. If you're regularly connecting, through whatever means is right for you, setting your actions should be effortless and easy. The universe provides the clues you need to follow, but you must be awake in order to pick them up.

Create a support network

It's important to create a network of people around you who can help you along on your journey. So whom do you know who may help you attain your goals? Go through your mobile phone, your e-mail address book or old diaries and see who in your network has the potential to assist you. Maybe it's an old work colleague who now works in a field similar to the one you want to move into. Perhaps a friend who works for a newspaper can get you the publicity you need, or maybe you know someone who has just been on a workshop that would be perfect for you. Open your eyes and look around you: you'll be amazed at the resources you have at your fingertips. If you don't know anyone, ask around, look on the internet and make a few telephone calls. Reading a good book may also be a tremendous source of support. I have read some truly amazing books and without the wisdom of their authors I wouldn't be where I am today.

Become accountable

This is an extremely important component of getting to where you want to be. How many of us have real accountability in our lives? Most of us stopped being answerable to anyone the day we hung up our school uniforms for the last time. Let's face it. We are a nation of procrastinators. If there is no one to push us forwards we remain within our comfort zone, where it is nice and safe. Once I had a taskmaster of a boss; he always had his beady eye on me, watching my every move, and making sure I was working to my full capacity. Although I absolutely hated this at the time there is no doubt whatsoever that I worked harder when he was in the office. When he went out, which he did frequently, I'd slow down my pace considerably. Funny that! It's just like having a personal trainer. When you have someone standing by your side encouraging and pushing you, you're more likely to do 50 bench presses than 30!

I'm not suggesting that you find someone who can berate you every time you find yourself dragging your feet, but a good healthy dose of accountability will certainly help you achieve far greater things and, more importantly, you'll reach your goals much more quickly. This is exactly why coaching works so well. A 1998 survey by the International Coaching Federation revealed that 98.5%

of clients polled reported their investment in coaching to be highly valuable. The general feedback from clients was that using a coach enabled them to become incredibly focused and therefore produce results faster. Accountability works!

It's time to create your 'coaching buddy'. To whom can you become accountable? Having someone impartial, like a life coach or mentor, is always advantageous but I understand that this isn't always an option for everyone so consider a family member, colleague or good friend. Choose your coaching buddy carefully as you need someone who will support you fully and not water down your plan. The job of your coaching buddy is to:

- Give you undivided support at all times.
- Praise you when things go well.
- Encourage you when you hit obstacles.
- Commit to having a weekly conversation with you to ensure that you are keeping on track.
- Celebrate your successes with you.

To get your coaching buddy to 'buy-in' to your goals you need to tell him, or her, your overall plan and what you expect from them. He or she needs to know exactly what their role is in helping you achieve your goals. You must make this clear or you will be disappointed when they don't meet your expectations.

Keep the excitement alive

When you're working on a particular goal for a lengthy period there will, without doubt, be times when you will hit a 'wall' and this will dent your enthusiasm somewhat. You are not alone. Everyone has to navigate his or her way through the jungle and occasionally you will get smacked in the face by a thorny branch. We all carry the scars to prove this. Each time this happens it can deplete your energy, leaving you feeling deflated and disappointed. You will hit blocks so get used to it but do not let them dilute your excitement and fervour. You must keep your dream alive, no matter what!

When you have a bad day and feel your excitement dwindling, do something that reconnects you with your original dream. When I am working towards a particular goal I make sure I visualise the final outcome everyday as this ensures that my focus is where it needs to be and away from any setbacks or obstacles. If you allow yourself to be affected by setbacks it will snuff out your enthusiasm, which perpetually leads you to procrastinate and take no further action. Think of ways to keep your excitement alive.

One client, when she felt she was moving off-base, would visit her local car dealership and sit in the car she intended to buy herself when she'd achieved her goals. Simple, but it made the world of difference to her mind-set. She told me that she would always come away with a renewed sense of vigour and drive.

Another client created a 'vision board' full of pictures from magazines that represented the life she would be living once she had achieved her goals. She used colourful images of beautiful landscapes, her ideal home and garden, and a picture of a happy family. She made her vision board as emotive as she possibly could so every time she looked at it she felt joyful and reconnected to her goals. It reminded her why she set then in the first place.

When you feel your excitement deteriorating ask yourself: 'What can I do immediately to lift my mood?' (For example, go for a walk, put on my favourite music or contact my coaching buddy.)

Don't tell the world

Remember, when you start making big changes to your life people start to notice – and most of them don't like it. This is because it highlights their own inability to transform their own lives. Don't be upset by this, it is human nature. We compare ourselves to others, and this is always going to be futile. This is why it is imperative to have a coaching buddy or a support network to call on. Someone who can share your dreams with you so you don't feel you have to tell every Tom, Dick and Harry about them to get the support you need. If you have had a bad day you don't whinge at everyone. Share your frustration with your coaching buddy, your support network or your Inner Guide.

Keep your dreams to yourself, and don't tell the world. Other people will only add their 'two-penneth' and, in the process, steal a little bit of your positive energy. There is nothing better than accomplishing a goal completely and then announcing it to the world – it's an awesome feeling! Perhaps think of it as being in the early stages of your first pregnancy and keep 'hush-hush' until you've reached the safe zone of 12 weeks. Think how wonderful it is to walk around knowing you have such a special secret. It feels incredible! There is something magical about keeping your intentions and dreams to yourself, and then announcing them when you're absolutely ready.

Clear out the rubbish

Before we start getting into action I want you to get your house in order. How can you expect to be focused if your physical environment is filled with clutter? As the saying goes, 'A clear house equals a clear mind'. If you're consistently looking at unfinished DIY or have a cascade of crumpled clothes fall on your head each time you open the wardrobe door, it's only going to add to your stress levels and take your attention away from where it needs to be.

Make an inventory of your house or office and list all the jobs that you've been putting off for months, or even years. Are there unused clothes in the spare room? Are there piles of old DVDs, books, paperwork, old letters and bills cluttering up your shelves or cupboards? If so it's time to clear them out, once and for all. Remember, this is the start to your new life so what better time to tackle it? You never know, you might even raise some cash to help fund your goals.

Exercise

Make a list of ten niggly jobs you need to do and put the list on the fridge door! Spend the weekend or a few evenings sorting these jobs out, once and for all. Get some help if you need to, but get them done.

Time to get into action!

Before you do anything else I want you to do one of the following.

- Buy a diary.
- Create a coaching folder.
- Buy a journal.

I want you to have a book to keep all your ideas, strategies and actions in one place. The last things you need are scraps of paper all over your house. It's time to get organised! If you've never been the organised type, now is the time to start. Take a trip to your local stationers and buy all the equipment you think you're going to need. It doesn't have to be expensive; a cardboard folder will keep everything in one place.

Looking at each of your goals in turn, write a list of potential contacts or supports that you have at your fingertips. Perhaps friends, an old boss, good books, workshops, seminars, local resources such as your library, and so on. List anyone or anything that will help you bring about your goals.

Recruit your coaching buddy

Make a list of five potential coaching buddies. Once you have done this write down three advantages and three disadvantages for each person. Evaluate and make your final decision as to who is the best person for the job.

Your very first action is to phone your selected coaching buddy and advise them about your plans. Share your goals, tell your buddy about this book and ask whether he or she is prepared and committed to help you on your passage to your new life. If they agree, suggest that you get together for a coffee so you can make a start.

Write the name of your chosen coaching buddy here

_____

The date of your first meeting is

_____

Exercise
Create your strategies

It's time to create your strategy for each goal. Use a blank piece of paper and brainstorm all the major areas you think you'll need to cover in order to reach each of your goals. Don't worry about their order at this stage: just list everything that comes to mind. You're looking for between three and eight strategies for each of your goals. If you find you have a list of nine or more, refine and amalgamate your list until you have no more than eight. Once you have done this put them into a logical order and write down your final list. This is the plan you will be following from now until you achieve your goals.

Exercise
Start creating your actions

Unlike strategies, you simply cannot map out every action you're going to take in advance. It's impossible. Your actions must remain fluid as they will change on an almost daily basis. As new ideas and insight flow into your consciousness your actions will inevitably alter, and this is exactly as it should be. To begin setting your actions you need to take your first strategy for each goal and think of approximately four or five small steps which you can take to kickstart your goals in the right direction.

Now write your first five actions for each of your three goals.

Well done! You're off the starting block. It's important that you now ensure you take time to complete each and every step. No procrastinating, as this will just slow things down. If you find yourself postponing your action, ask yourself why. What limiting belief is sabotaging your success? Imagine how wonderful you'll feel when you get to the end of the week having achieved all 15 actions – fantastic, I promise.

But it doesn't end there! Now you've got the ball rolling *it is essential* that you sit down at the same time every week and re-evaluate each of your actions, and then set brand-new ones to take your goal forwards to the next stage. This is how the process must work if you want to succeed. Be sure to recognise your achievements and give yourself a good old pat on the back.

Exercise

How will you celebrate your successes?

As you travel along the path of success it's important that you praise yourself for all your achievements: because if you don't, no one else will. Write down every success that you have – from a simple phone call to securing a new contract. Remember, when you do this you are creating solid evidence that will help you to form a healthy mind-set which will ensure you make it to the winning line. Evidence list aside, I also recommend that every time you complete each strategy you find a way of celebrating your accomplishments, either on your own, with family or with your coaching buddy.

Here are some suggestions:
- buy yourself a treat, maybe a new book or a new handbag
- open a bottle of bubbly
- pamper yourself: have a back massage or your favourite beauty treatment
- go out to your favourite café or restaurant for something to eat
- do something you've always wanted to, such as ice-skating or a singing lesson, parachuting, hot air ballooning, going on an assault course or spa weekend away.

Now list ten ways you will celebrate your successes.

Exercise
Your self belief

What do you need to believe for each of your goals to manifest? Your beliefs play a huge part in achieving or failing to achieve your goals. If you do not adopt the right mind-set you will fall short and your journey will be fraught. For each of your three goals, write down (in the present tense) three new beliefs that you must start working on in order for you to change your mind-set and, ultimately, triumph.

It's not enough for your beliefs just to be written in your notebook, diary, journal or whatever method you're using. You need to see your new beliefs every single day. Write down each new belief on a Post-it® note three or four times and stick the notes around the house. The bathroom mirror is always a good place or how about the inside of your wardrobe door, your car dashboard, your kitchen cupboards or computer? Make sure you affirm these new beliefs as often as you can.

Exercise

Excitement boosters

It's vital to keep your excitement alive. It will naturally ebb and flow, but you need to keep the overall passion burning. Don't allow the flame to go out. List five ways you intend to keep your excitement alive, from creating a vision board to mixing with successful people or visiting a particular place.

Exercise

Your daily workout

This book is about finding a whole new way of living, and if you truly want to achieve your goals you are going to have to start doing things differently. If you continue to live your life as you have always done you will keep getting the same results. It's as simple as that. I have given you all the tools you need to help you generate the life you want to lead, but the buck stops here. It's over to you now.

If you want to succeed it's time to change, once and for all. I want you to create a daily mental workout that will ensure you cannot fail.

Here's an example:

- *7 am* Visualise my day in advance, seeing everything going the way I want.
- *7.30 am* Whilst in shower repeat positive affirmations, ten times each.
- *8.30 am* Whilst driving listen to an inspiration audiotape.
- *12.30 pm* Spend lunch-hour working on actions steps.
- *3 pm* Take five minutes to repeat positive affirmation, ten times each.
- *5 pm* Whilst driving home listen to an inspiration audiotape.
- *5.30 pm* Continue working on actions steps.
- *6.30 pm* Spend 20 minutes meditating and visualising future.
- *11 pm* Before going to sleep repeat affirmations one final time, recapping on the successes of my day. If anything didn't quite go to plan visualise how I would have wanted it to go instead.

Start right now!

What are you waiting for?

Madelyn's story

Madelyn was an outgoing type: very bubbly with a quick wit and a sense of humour. She was in her mid-forties and lived with her husband and two cats in north London. Madelyn's primary goal was to build her own home in the West Country. She'd worked in London as an interior designer for many years and had always vowed that she wanted a more simple life away from the smog of the big city. She and her husband had decided they wanted to build their own eco-friendly cottage before they both reached 50, where they could live a self-sustainable existence, rearing animals and growing their own vegetables – a far cry from life in north London! When she came to me Madelyn had three years in which to bring her life-long dream to fruition and she had realised that she needed to get cracking if she was to reach her target.

Madelyn openly admitted that she was a 'scatty' type, very disorganised and a complete procrastinator. She was great at creating wonderful designs and interiors for everyone else, yet when it came to her own life she never seemed to have time or take the actions necessary to bring own her personal dreams and ideas to fruition. Her friends and family were sick of hearing about her zany and innovative ideas, but never really took much notice of them as they were used to them not materialising. This made Madelyn feel unsupported and this only encouraged her to procrastinate further. She was determined that this had to stop: her eco-friendly cottage was an absolute must and an opportunity to prove to herself and to those around her that she could do it. But she needed help!

Madelyn not only required a good measure of accountability, she also needed a firm strategy and an action plan if she was to make her vision into reality. Once we had established her goal, which was to 'buy land and draw up plans for my beautiful new home in the West Country', we then created a solid action plan containing six key milestones. Once we had these two vital components, Madelyn was ready to take action.

The first thing I encouraged her to do was to go out and buy a new diary, which could be used solely for achieving her goal. Each week Madelyn would write herself a 'To do' list (something she'd never done previously) with 15 new actions to be taken that week. She would then prioritise these actions and plan them into her weekly schedule. This made a huge difference to Madelyn, as for the first time in her life she felt like she had a structure to follow and felt like she was actually getting somewhere.

It was amazing just how much progress she was making just by setting 15 actions per week. Having me as her coaching buddy gave Madelyn the accountability she needed so that she didn't fall into the procrastination trap. Her dream was rapidly becoming real, and this gave Madelyn the drive, determination and passion to keep pushing forwards. Once Madelyn was off there was no stopping her. She was like a new woman!

Approximately six months later Madelyn found a perfect piece of land in beautiful, quaint village a few miles from the coast, and she hired an architect to start working on the design for her dream home. Madelyn is now only months away from relocating.

The key to achieving any big goal is getting organised and being disciplined.

Chapter 8

Facing your fears

So what happens when you've created your magnificent life-changing goals, you've mapped out your strategies and you've even signed up your coaching buddy, and you find yourself hiding in a cupboard, paralysed by fear and unable to peek outside? What do you do then?

In this final chapter I will show you how to face your fears head on and how to bounce back with vigour and determination.

Let's get one thing clear – everyone has fears, some small and some big. Some of us fear getting it wrong, looking like an idiot, changing jobs, losing our relationship, getting old, public speaking, swimming or even being a bad parent. We all have something we fear at some level.

It's human nature. We are programmed to be fearful of the unknown.

In this day and age we are conditioned to fear everything from a spider on the floor to the world at large. We fear change, we fear beginnings, we fear endings, we fear living and we even fear dying. Fear may be all-consuming, immense and debilitating that it keeps you stuck within your comfort zone for decades without ever moving forwards. The more time that passes the worse the fear gets. You end up living your life in limbo, feeling disappointed, prodded and let down by life. Life in the shadow of fear is a horrible place to reside. You must not let fear rob you of the opportunity to succeed and grow in life. I often tell my clients that if they are not fearful they are not progressing or growing. Fear is just a clear sign that we've reached the edge of our comfort zone. The question is: 'Will you jump off into the unknown or run back?'

What people don't realise is that fear is a normal part of life, and it is essential if you want to live to your true potential.

Fear is encapsulated within goal-setting. When you venture into new territory you will come face to face with your own personal demons. The key is not to run as fast as you can in the opposite direction, but to face fear head on, and, believe me, it's never as bad as you think it's going to be.

I almost allowed fear to sabotage my dreams was when I signed up to my life-coach training programme. It had been a long time since I'd done any type of formal training and I was petrified at the thought of doing assignments and taking exams. Would I be able to keep up? Would I like the people I was training with? What would happen if I didn't pass? What if I realised coaching wasn't my dream after all? I remember my train pulling into Euston Station on a frosty cold January morning. It was the first day of my training programme. As I looked around the carriage I wondered what everyone else was doing in London: were they here to work, to see family, to shop? As I stood up and approached the train door I could feel the palms of my hands become more and more sweaty. I gripped the handle of my little weekend bag for extra comfort trying to imagine it was my husband's hand instead. It didn't work. What was I doing! It was the first time I had been to London alone and I could feel the panic start to take hold of my body. My chest tightened and my breathing became shallow. I remember thinking that maybe I could just spend the weekend shopping instead. Who would know? As I stepped off the train, I joined the frenzied commuters all trying to make their way to the exit. Even with hundreds of people walking to my left and right I had never quite felt so lonely. I could have cried. It would have been so easy to have jumped on the next train home and forgot all about my dreams of starting a new career. When I got out of the station the cold winter sunshine hit my colourless face and I immediately felt better. I flagged down a black cab (I wasn't going attempt the Tube, oh no) and made my way to the venue. As the morning progressed my fear slowly subsided. I met some of the most amazing people that weekend, and the memory of the experience stays firmly locked within my mind as one of the major achievements in my career thus far.

Remember, each time you face a fear your comfort zone expands and, in turn, so does your life.

When we feel an emotion that is uncomfortable, such as fear, many of us tend to run away or push it aside, often by distracting ourselves with food, TV, the internet and so on, or simply by swallowing the feeling and continuing to live our lives in the shadow of fear. When you find that nothing seems to ease the apprehension, embrace it instead of resisting your feelings. It's OK to be fearful, it's a natural part of life, it means you're growing; it means that you've made a decision to move forwards. Experience the fear and let it move through your body. Remember, it's never as bad as you think it's going to be!

Every successful person has felt fear on his or her journey to a better life. It's part of the course and unavoidable so you need to get used to it.

Often we subconsciously do things when we're scared to avoid having to deal with the fear we're facing. Here are some common signs to look out for.

* Rather than take a specific action you find yourself looking for distractions or new projects, you start clearing out cupboards you haven't touched for ten years or redecorating your bedroom.
* You start phoning every friend in your phonebook.
* You start watching TV or listening to the radio more.
* You find yourself constantly checking your favourite social networking website.
* You find yourself eating more.
* You feel apathetic and tired.
* You get cross when anyone asks how you are getting on with your goals.

- You find yourself taking the dog for a walk six times a day.
- You volunteer to stay late at work or work the weekend.
- You get involved in other people's crises.
- You find yourself being very negative and pessimistic.
- You avoid the all calls from your coaching buddy!

Get comfortable with failure

If you are going to make it to the finishing line you have to be comfortable with the idea of failing. In most cases it's not the actual failing that's terrifying, it's the *fear of failing* that really paralyses people. You must understand that fear is just an emotion. Feelings are all the same, whether you're happy, sad, angry or frightened. They are only emotions and not something from outside. Feelings are derived from the thoughts you hold and the images that you play out in your mind, so in order to change your feelings it makes sense that you change the thoughts and images in your head. When you feel scared it's normally because you have allowed your Inner Critic to consume your mind with negative thoughts! Whenever your Inner Critic has an opportunity to pounce on you and prove that your original negative beliefs are true, it will do. It'll say, 'When are you going to stop kidding yourself and get back to your "real" life?' or 'Stop fooling yourself, you know you'll never succeed.' Your Inner Critic will sabotage your success at every opportunity if you let it.

When you find yourself consumed by the harmful voice of your Inner Critic and totally rooted to the spot with terror, it's a clear sign that it's time to tune into your Inner Guide. Change the pictures in your mind, or the thoughts in your head, to something more positive. It's up to you to take control. If your mind is powerful enough to make you feel down, conversely, it is also powerful enough to make you feel good; it's just a state of mind. Remember, all emotions are the same; we decide which are good or bad.

Life is too short to be afraid. You need to cultivate the mind-set of the truly successful. They, too, feel fear, but they have learnt how to turn their trepidation to their advantage and use fear to propel them forwards. Let others plod through life; it's time to get serious about living the life you really want.

It's only feedback!

One vital piece of advice I received when starting my journey was that *failure is simply feedback*. Think about it for a second: failing is just feedback! It doesn't mean it's the end of the road, or that it's time to give up. It's a pointer to prompt you to change direction. This critical bit of information helped me to turn the concept of failure completely on its head.

Look at it like this. When something goes wrong, if you don't get the deal you were banking on or if someone turns you down for a date you were looking forwards to, instead of seeing it as a failure, or the end of story, see it as feedback from the universe or your Inner Guide telling you to try a different route. When something in my own life doesn't go according to plan, rather than beating myself up for days on end and allowing myself to become downhearted I think 'OK, that obviously wasn't the best path to follow, there must be something better on the horizon'. I then let go of all judgement and wait for fresh inspiration to flow into my consciousness. And, amazingly, it always does, and the new ideas are always far better.

At one point I hit a major roadblock and the feeling of failure nearly sabotaged a lifelong dream. What seemed like complete failure at the time turned out to be a wonderful blessing in disguise. I had started my new life-coaching business whilst I was still in full-time employment. Needless to say, it was hard work working from 9 am to 5 pm and then having to come home and start my second job. But at the time it was necessary as, of course, it is for most people when they are starting out. I thought I was superwoman and could do it all: hold down a job; be a good mother; run a home; and, on top of all these, start a new business. Things were fine for a time but it wasn't going to be sustainable, even though I thought it was. Something had to give. On top of all that I decided it would be a great idea to get pregnant! Yes, I know. I must have been living in 'La-La land'. But I had what I thought was a perfectly timed 'Grand Plan'. I would have the baby, go on maternity leave and enjoy the time with my new baby whilst growing my new life-coaching practice. After my maternity leave (when I had lots of new clients in the bag) I would inform my employer I wouldn't be returning to work, giving me the perfect lifestyle that I was desperately seeking. What a great opportunity to build my business without having to take any risks at all! I had it all mapped out. What I failed to do at the time was listen to my Inner Guide. I ignored all guidance or gut feeling I had and simply followed my logic, and took what I thought would be the best and easiest route. And because life was so hectic at the time I rarely found a moment for meditation or visualising. I had completely lost my spiritual connection.

This was to be futile. Three months into my pregnancy I lost my baby unexpectedly and, as you can imagine, it was a horrible shock. Not only did I lose my baby, I almost lost my own life as well as I had a huge haemorrhage and was rushed into hospital. Not a pleasant experience I can tell you. The weeks that followed were spent in bed wallowing in self-pity. I had failed. My Grand Plan had failed and I felt as if my world had collapsed around me. I didn't know which way to turn. I tried to work out why it had happened, but I just felt as if I had a dense fog clouding my vision. I had lost my clarity. It wasn't until a few months later that the fog finally lifted and it all became very clear indeed.

Going through such a traumatic experience forced me to re-evaluate my life. It helped me to make some huge life-changing decisions. Subsequently I was able to see what a fool I had been, allowing myself to take on so much pressure. Shortly after this I handed in my notice and went self-employed. I'm sure I wouldn't have made this decision without having gone through my so-called 'failure'. The blessings that have come out of this have been incredible. Later on, after spending lots of quality time growing my new life-coaching practice, I fell pregnant again and went on to have a healthy baby boy.

You may or may not experience such traumas on your journey (I certainly hope not!). But when things go wrong we need to listen – it's vital feedback. I had plenty of feedback along the way, I just ignored it. I thought I knew best and stopped listening to my Inner Guide. Remember, feedback comes in lots of different ways. It may be a missed train, a cancelled meeting or a rejection of some kind. *Failure is simply feedback and an opportunity to step back and look at your situation with fresh eyes.* When you can do this you'll see the real truth of your situation.

Dealing with knockbacks

There will be knockbacks from time to time. There will be times when you think to yourself 'I can't do this anymore!' I haven't met anyone who hasn't had to deal with some kind of obstacle on their way to the finishing line. The key is how you deal with knock-backs. The truly successful pick themselves up, dust themselves down and carry on. However, most of us don't do this and we use knock-backs as proof that our original negative belief ('I can't do this') was right all along. We use it as evidence that we were deluding ourselves and then we woefully retreat back into our comfort zone. The more we do this the stronger becomes the belief that we are incapable of making changes to our lives. Eventually we don't even try to attempt anything new because we expect to fall flat on our faces. And because we expect to fall short we invariably do!

Below are two examples of remarkable human beings, who when faced with huge setbacks decided not to call it a day. Instead they laughed in the face of adversity and went on to achieve remarkable things.

At the age of just 13 Bethany Hamilton was an aspiring surfing star. On the morning of 31 October 2003 Bethany and a few friends went out surfing as they usually did:
'I was lying on my board, parallel to the waves. One of my arms was lying in the water and the other was just holding the board. Then the shark just came up and attacked me, and it kind of pulled me back and forth. It was only, like, two or three seconds, so it was really quick.'

Bethany lost her entire left arm. Did she let this major knock-back stop her? No. Within six months she was surfing again, and winning.

Ray Kroc started McDonald's at the age of 52, when he realised that people didn't want to dine in any more, but would eat 'on the run' instead. At the time Ray Kroc had diabetes, lost his gall bladder and most of his thyroid gland. But he had a clear conviction that the best was ahead of him. And the rest, as they say, is history!

If these two remarkable people can pick themselves up and carry on, so can you. Yes, you will be disappointed when you are rejected, turned down or refused, but remember: it's only feedback and an opportunity to consider taking a different direction. See it for the blessing it really is.

As the great Greek philosopher, Epictotus, once said, 'It's not what happens to you, but how you react to it that matters.'

There have been lots of roadblocks on my journey, but there have also been many wonderful blessings that wouldn't have come about if it weren't for these so-called obstructions. Sometimes I did find it hard to scrape my flattened ego off the floor and start again, but I did it. It didn't feel great but I was on a huge learning curve and

I made sure I never repeated my mistakes. When I work with clients, part of my job is to support them when they feel as if they have been hit by a truck and are left feeling completely bewildered. This is why it's so important to have a coaching buddy to give you the support you need when things go wrong. It can make all the difference. When we don't have support it's easy to pretend we've done all that we can and just give up.

The key is to pick yourself up as quickly as possible and continue on your way: when you fall off your horse you should get straight back on again. Do not linger as this will only make things appear worse. Find a way that makes you feel better. We'll look at how to do this shortly.

So let me ask you how you will choose to respond to the challenges before you? Will you give up, like you have always done, or this time will you be a fighter and forge on?

Don't take 'No' for an answer!

One thing I have become fascinated with over recent years is what makes some individuals more successful than others. Why do some become people super-rich yet others don't have two pennies to rub together? What do they do differently? Of course, a lot has to do with adopting the right mind-set, but another important ingredient to being successful is persistence. Tenacity plays a huge role in whether or not you achieve your goals.

I met a multi-millionaire around the time I was about to leave my job to go self-employed. By chance I happened to be sitting in his office, along with a friend. I'd never met a multi-millionaire before and I was rather curious. As I looked around the office all I could see was evidence of this man's achievements. There were placards on the walls displaying awards that he'd won, and there were pictures of him mingling with the world's rich and famous, not to mention a glass-topped table and a the biggest wide-screen TV I'd ever seen mounted on the far wall. It was another world, and I wanted to know how he'd created it.

Some people might have felt inferior surrounded by his success and opulence; I was fascinated. What made this man so successful? I needed to know.

As we sat talking I had an impulse to ask him what his secret was. I knew that if I walked out of his office I wouldn't get the opportunity again. I waited for a break in the conversation and, ignoring my pounding heart and the screams of my Inner Critic, asked, 'You're obviously a very successful man and I'm just about to set up my own company. Would you mind me asking, what is the secret to your success?' My friend looked at me in horror. We were here to discuss a contract we were working on at the time and I had dared to bring my personal life into the conversation. Obviously she thought I'd lost the plot and was about to get both of us fired.

He turned to me with a twinkle in his eyes. I knew what he was thinking. I'd never been the quiet type and had always firmly believed (and still do) that if you don't ask, you don't get! Giving me a warm smile he said, very calmly, 'Above all: don't give up. Don't be scared to go where you think others have already been before you. BE PERSISTENT until you get what you want.' He smiled again and I knew without doubt he respected my nerve for asking the question. I had it! I had the answer and I felt great. I decided at that point that 'persistence' was to become my new mantra.

There have been many occasions when I have put this advice to good use. When I started my new business, like so many others, I had little money for advertising. I specifically recall sitting at my dining table one wet and dreary Sunday afternoon trying to brainstorm ways to attract new customers. Then the brainwave struck. I knew from past experience that newspapers and magazines were always looking for interesting stories to fill their pages. If I could get a regular column, or even a one-off feature, people would read it and I could start to get my message out. Free advertising! So I sat down that evening and wrote my very first article. Then came the hard bit: on the Monday morning I started researching relevant magazines, both locally and regionally, and started to e-mail my article to them. I sent 25 e-mails that day and no one responded. No, that's a lie. I had three responses, all saying, 'Thank you, but no thank you.' I felt flat as a pancake. At this point most people would give up, convincing themselves that they had tried very hard but it wasn't going to work. But, at this point you should see your so-called setback as vital feedback – and try a different route instead. And this is what I did. I knew if I could get my face into some magazines clients would start flowing in. So the next day, after spending all morning procrastinating, drinking endless cups of tea and making unnecessary calls to friends, I finally plucked up the courage to contact some of the editors I had e-mailed the previous day. Much to my surprise they were very pleasant and said they would keep my details on file. I didn't get a 'yes' that day, but I moved the parameters of my comfort zone a little and it felt good. Over the months that followed I made a point of e-mailing these editors each and every time I wrote a new article and, within six months, I had regular features in five magazines. What I result! If I hadn't been persistent and had given up at the first hurdle I wouldn't have been encouraged to write for bigger magazines and eventually write this book! The moral of this story is: *do not take 'No' for an answer!*

Learn from the best

I think if any of us were to sit down with an entrepreneur or an Olympic gold medallist, they would all say that their journey to a better life was not easy, nor painless. These individuals achieve amazing things by refusing to be put off. They have a clear vision of where they are going and let nothing deter them.

The rags-to-riches story of J K Rowling is a fascinating one. The idea for Harry Potter was first born whilst she was commuting from her home in Manchester to London each day. J K Rowling started working on her book, but was suddenly cast into the role of single mother; her life altered and she had to move back to Scotland where she found herself surviving on welfare benefits. But J K Rowling continued to pursue her dream of writing a children's book. Eventually she finished her manuscript and sent it off to a publisher, only for it to be rejected. But, J K Rowling didn't see this as the end of the road; she simply tried again until a publisher agreed to take on her work.

As we all know, when *Harry Potter and the Philosopher's Stone* was published in 1997 it was an instant success with both children and adults alike. J K Rowling's tale is an astonishing reversal of fortune: from welfare mum to one of the most recognized authors on the planet.

Another inspiring story is that of Jim Carrey. Jim had to drop out of high school to take a job as a janitor in a factory, along with the rest of his family. But Jim had a passion for comedy and had a clear picture of what he wanted from life. He actually wrote himself a $10 million cheque as a reminder of his inevitable future success. After working on the comedy circuit for many years he landed his first role in *Living Color*. After this Jim moved into bigger film roles. His hits included *Ace Ventura*, *The Mask* and *Dumb and Dumber*, to name but a few, and Jim Carrey became one of the highest-paid comedians and actors in Hollywood history.

Did you know that it took James Dyson 5127 prototypes, 14 years of debt and multiple lawsuits to create the top-selling upright vacuum cleaner? Or that it took Thomas Edison over 3000 attempts to create the light bulb? When he was asked about the failures he said, 'I didn't fail 3000 times; I found 3000 ways how not to create a light bulb.' What a great mind-set! What I'm trying to demonstrate is that the vast majority of overnight successes really took a lot longer; it's just that we don't know their full story. Just like us, successful people have had to work hard, make difficult decisions and have undoubtedly come up against blockages that have altered the course of their path.

We have to understand that failure is just part of life when achieving big goals? If you remain steadfast to your original vision you will succeed. Turn yourself into someone who is totally solution-focused. As soon as obstacles present themselves make a commitment to yourself to find a better way, because when you do this, you will be shown a new way, I promise.

Self-sabotage

One thing I want you to become aware of, especially now that you're in the process of setting your weekly action steps, is your unique self-sabotaging style. By 'sabotage' I mean subconscious behaviours, or habits, that you perform which slow down your progress or stop you moving forwards altogether. Your self-sabotaging style is always derived from your innermost fears of failing. We all have a self-sabotaging style, and some of us have more than one. They are familiar long-standing behaviours that you put in place many moons ago as a safely mechanism. Just like your Inner Critic, you need to become aware of their existence. Because once you are aware of them you will be able to see them for what they really are and quickly move on, instead of letting them hold you back. Remember, awareness is the key.

I realised my own self-sabotaging style early on, and I was astonished at the harmful impact I allowed it to have on my life. My style was procrastination. As always I would form my weekly 'to do' list and what I found myself doing was putting the easiest jobs at the top of my list and the more challenging jobs at the bottom. This invariably meant I would never get round to my more difficult tasks. Of course it felt great every time I crossed yet another small action off my list, but I was just kidding myself as none of the bigger, more challenging actions was ever reached. I found myself rewriting these more difficult items on my 'to do' list week after week.

Basically, if anything was outside my comfort zone I would find something that would distract me from having to take action. I'd eat; I'd call my mum for a chat. I'd pop to the shops or decide it was a good time to re-organise my kitchen cupboards. I'd be delighted if the phone rang as this was the ultimate distraction and the perfect excuse to not take action. I'd then realise 'Oh dear it's 5 pm, I'll have to do it tomorrow.' And the story repeated itself until I brought my self-sabotaging style to light and finally put an end to it. I say 'put an end to it', but, just like your Inner Critic, it will pop up when you least expect it. Even now I find myself falling into the procrastination trap and I have to pull myself out quickly before it takes hold. On many occasions whilst writing this book I'd find myself delaying action, especially when I found a particular section difficult or more challenging to write. I would tell myself I needed another chocolate biscuit, even though I'd just eaten one, anything that would delay action and extinguish my fear of failure. It's safer not to take action as this means you'll never have to deal with rejection. But this means you live your live in limbo, never really moving forwards.

Other people have quite different styles of sabotage. Some individuals are perfectionists. They'll fixate on one route and insist that's the only way. They'll perform whatever it is they are working on at least a hundred times before they're happy and satisfied with it. It has to be faultless or they don't take any action whatsoever. This means things rarely get finished; they always have endless lists of unfinished tasks, from DIY to personal projects. Much like procrastination, perfectionism has its own drawbacks and, if you let it, will interfere with your goals.

When I work with my clients over a period of time I start to notice their self-sabotaging styles. Of course, no one really likes to be told about their flaws, but it's important to be aware of them if you want to achieve big things in life. Below I have listed (in my experience) the top six sabotaging styles.

- *Procrastination*: – delaying action, insisting other things must take precedence before goals can be progressed.
- *Perfectionism*: keeping re-doing something because it must be perfect, but in doing so we never seem to move any closer to our goals.
- *Dreaming*: blissfully spending our time dreaming about how wonderful life will be when we achieve

our goals. We create wonderful plans, lists and mood boards, but never take any real action.

- *Laziness*: we expect everyone around us to take action for us and won't take any action ourselves.
- *Blaming others*: we won't take responsibility and blame everyone else for our past failures or inaction.
- *Being an airhead*: being disorganised and running around, never seeming to make progress. Airheads never move any closer to their goals because they're always too busy dealing with one crisis or another.

Exercise
Answer the following questions.

- How do you best sabotage yourself?
- What kind of things do you do when you are in this style?
- How does this affect your progress?

So what's the solution? Well, unfortunately, there isn't a magic pill that will miraculously cure you of your self-sabotaging. Just like your Inner Guide and Inner Critic, you simply need to become aware of it. Once you are conscious of your preferred self-sabotaging style you can change your behaviour to something more advantageous. Notice when you fall into your sabotaging style and do the opposite to what you'd normally do. Again, this is why it pays to have a coaching buddy as others will notice your self-sabotaging style far better than you do yourself. When I find myself procrastinating around a certain action I don't chastise myself, I simply laugh at myself instead and say 'Caught you!' We're great at kidding ourselves that we're making headway even though we're just going round and round in circles, going nowhere, fast. Be aware!

Re-address your beliefs

When you find it impossible to get out of the habit of sabotaging yourself it's time to re-address your beliefs once again. When a long-standing belief is deep-routed your Inner Critic will do its utmost to keep you tied to it, no matter what. If you find this is the case it's time to look again at your limiting beliefs and start practising the exercises we've already spoken about the in the previous chapters. When we sabotage ourselves it's because we are still running an old negative belief, and the best way to change an old belief is to feel the fear and carry out the action we're terrified of doing. When we do this we are not only expanding our comfort zone we are also programming the mind with a 'can do' attitude. When I ask clients what is getting in the way of them moving forwards many of them recall times in their life when they have failed. This is a clear sign that some old programming is still running. Thinking about past failures is a sure fire way to shoot yourself in the foot, and is certainly not helpful! This is why it is essential to address your negative beliefs and start doing something about them.

Bouncing back from adversity

Having worked with hundreds of people who have made enormous life changes, and having made some extensive changes to my own life, I have come to realise that sometimes we all need time to take stock of where we are before we can find the energy to move on. And there is absolutely nothing wrong with this, as long as we don't stay still for too long!

There have been days when I have experienced a particular setback which has left me feeling flummoxed, and I've decided that the best thing to do is to shut my laptop, put on my pyjamas and watch my favourite film. Remember, you cannot make a silk purse from a sow's ear: taking action from a negative space will always be futile. People smell fear and they feel your anxiety! When you feel pessimistic it is better to take no action at all then to take action derived from fear or panic. Obviously the children still need to be picked up from school or the food needs to be bought. I'm not talking about this kind of action. I'm talking about 'inspired' action. When we're fearful, apathetic or anxious it's never advisable to take new actions because the results won't be beneficial, thus adding to our plight. Always, always, wait until you feel strong again before you take your next step, that way you know the results will be in line with what you want. Remember how the Law of Attraction works.

Taking time out

When you feel as if you're at the edge of a 100-foot drop, and about to be pushed over the edge, or when your Inner Critic has completely saturated every good thought in your head, it's a clear sign to take some time out. Don't feel bad about this. We all need time out occasionally, it doesn't mean you're weak or on the road to ruin. It just means you need a little time to refill your energy tank. Just like your car you, too, cannot function if your energy tank is running dry. It's important to notice when this happens. So many of us fail to recognise the 'red light' in front our eyes and end up causing ourselves enormous turmoil. Here are some clear signs that you're in need of some time out.

- You don't seem to have time to eat or, worse still, go to the loo.
- You realise you haven't seen your wife or kids all week.
- You are consistently working till 10 pm every night.
- You're checking your e-mails every five minutes.
- You feel anxious and panicky all the time.
- You have not time to look after yourself or pursue your hobbies.
- You grab unhealthy snacks instead of preparing nutritious meals.
- You're using alcohol or cigarettes to relax you.
- You can't sleep because your head is spinning.
- You don't want to get out of bed in the morning.
- You look tired and worn out.
- You're always ill.

When you find you're experiencing any of the above, be kind to yourself, *stop what you are doing and take some much-needed time out,* because if you don't you'll miss some vital piece of the jigsaw and will inevitably be thrown off course. This is where I went wrong just before I had my miscarriage. I was experiencing all of the above signs: I was working all hours; I was using wine to help me relax at night; I was obsessed, and I mean totally obsessed, with checking my website stats and e-mails;

and the worst of it was I saw so little of my daughter I felt like I had custody of her for one or two hours a week! But I couldn't see any of this at the time. Others around me could, but I simply wouldn't listen. The universe was desperately trying to steer me away from impact but I couldn't hear the messages my Inner Guide was giving me and eventually it all ended in tears. I will never let this happen to me again. I have learnt my lesson. So, please, take heed and listen to your body and inner spirit because, when we are tuned in, we will be given all the directions we need to take our goals forwards.

Now, when I say 'time out' I'm not talking about taking a sabbatical. I'm not suggesting you to park your goals for a few months until you feel ready to carry on. Oh, no! I'm talking about a day, a few days – a week at most, just enough time to restore your energy levels. Sometimes just an early night, a good long walk or having a fun day out can make the world of difference. Have you ever noticed when you're away from your office, desk, computer or whatever, that ideas start to flow? You are inspired with new thoughts, things that you simply couldn't think previously? It really does pay to take time out.

Here are some examples of things you can do while talking time out.

- Spend the day in your comfy clothes or pyjamas and do *nothing*!
- Go for a long walk, alone or with your family.
- Spend time with nature, smell the roses; literally, appreciate life!
- Get your hands dirty in the garden.
- Spend the day with the kids doing off-the-wall things; give them 100%attention!
- Help out someone in need: a friend, a neighbour or family member; take your focus off yourself.
- Clear out your cupboards or garage.
- Repaint a room in your house in a new colour.
- Think about ways you can simplify your life, such as hiring a cleaner, hiring an accountant, doing your grocery shopping online, and so on.
- Read a good book or watch a DVD.
- Go away for the weekend.

Lower your sights

When you're feeling let down, disappointed or disillusioned a great remedy is to lower your sights somewhat. I don't mean revamp your entire goal and downscale it completely. What I'm suggesting is taking the smallest step you possibly can to move your goal forwards until you feel strong again. If you're overwhelmed, rather than letting your fear grind you to a halt entirely, take the tiniest step you can think of. Just taking one tiny step will feel a lot better than taking no action at all. For example, if you have been procrastinating for several days over making an important call to someone, break the action down. Perhaps send an e-mail beforehand, or leave a message asking them to call you. It doesn't matter how small your action, as long as you're moving forwards and not remaining motionless. When my clients fall into the procrastination trap I ask them, 'How can you change your action to make it seem less scary?' Sometimes we can be a little too ambitious with our actions because we're excited and keen to push ahead. There is nothing wrong with this, but, remember, high achievers take lots of little steps, not huge leaps or hurdles. Taking small steps or actions is without doubt the best route to achieving any goal. It's a bit like trying to lose weight. We all know that the most sensible way of shedding the pounds is by losing the weight slowly, maybe one or two pounds a week. When you lose too much too soon you invariably end up putting it all back on again and hence the yo-yo syndrome is born. If you're stuck, break your goal down into the smallest step you can possibly take and *do it now*! You'll not only get the wheels in motion again, you'll also feel fantastic in the process.

Focus on past successes

We discussed, in Chapter 3, how keeping a list of evidence is a great way of reprogramming your mind for success. But your evidence list will also come into its own when you find yourself unable to move. There is something very uplifting about looking back at your past successes. It's a superb way of helping you to get motivated and regain your gusto. It offers hard, undeniable proof that you are triumphant and able to accomplish remarkable things. So when you need a boost get out your evidence list, have yourself a coffee and a biscuit (or even two!) and celebrate your past successes.

Often my clients come to their session telling me they've had a really unproductive week and have not made much progress, in reality it's not the whole truth. When I probe a little further it usually turns out that they've made excellent headway but there have been one or two particular actions they didn't manage to achieve and they have allowed these to overshadow their overall progress. When I reel off a list of all their positive actions I see their face change as they realise they haven't been quite as unproductive as they originally thought. As human beings we so are hard on ourselves and habitually focus more on our so-called failures than we on our victories. If you find yourself being harsh, remind yourself of all your past successes; bring back the memory of the event, feel the feeling you felt at the time, let endorphins saturate your entire body until you feel powerful again.

Hand it over to spirit

This is probably one of the most powerful things you can do when you feel rooted to the spot by fear. Remember, achieving your goals in the mind alone isn't the best route; you can undoubtedly create wonderful things in your mind, but when you add a little dose of spirit your journey becomes a much smoother ride. Spirit is your ultimate fulfilment; it knows what you need; it knows what you want and, most importantly, it knows exactly how to get you there. But when we allow our minds to rule our daily lives, spirit cannot present itself to us and we miss out on the miracle. You do not have to work out everything yourself. You are not alone. There is a wonderful higher power lying dormant, right now, which you can call upon any time you need to. Why ignore this? It's like telling a pilot you want to fly the plane yourself when you're not a qualified pilot! If you find yourself feeling fearful, concerned, worried, anxious, frustrated, let down, apathetic, disappointed, upset or whatever – *hand over* and wait for the feeling to pass. Why hold on to feelings that are not going to serve you. When you let go, the issues or problems will dissolve into nothingness, quickly enabling you to move on.

When I feel stuck or negative, rather than trying to 'fix' the problem myself I have learnt to hand over and wait for fresh inspiration. I do this by simply meditating or quietening the mind using the techniques described in Chapter 6. As Einstein once said, '***You*** can never solve a ***problem*** on the level on which it was ***created.***'

Remember, your mind is programmed and is full of bad beliefs, concepts, thoughts, fears and perceptions which get in the way of you living the life you truly want. Yes, you can do affirmations, create evidence and the like, all these techniques undeniably work, but the more you can become aware of spirit the more harmonious and pleasurable your journey will become and the quicker things will start to change. In short, spirit can rewire your brain for you, if you let it.

So stop trying to fix the issues or problems in your life, raise your awareness heavenwards and remember you are a spiritual being. Life is actually *in*corporeal not corporeal, as we've all been led to believe. Once you recognise and start experiencing this, your fears will dissolve forever.

Where is all the money to come from?

We're nearly at the end of book, but there is one important element we haven't touched on – the dreaded issue of money! When we set out to make big life changes money invariably comes into the equation at some time or another. Whether it's money to retrain, travel or buy a particular item, most of us will need some extra cash at some point. In fact, this is probably one of the greatest excuses that people use for not making changes to their life. Most of us have mortgages, bills, loans, credit cards to pay and naturally these things can feel very stifling and restricting. Unfortunately, modern living has allowed us to live way beyond our means and of course this reduces our options in life because we become tied down by our own financial restraints. Just because you have this amazing new exciting goal to achieve doesn't mean you should run out and quit your job, or stop paying your bills, all these things still need to be maintained. As romantic as it may seem to just tell your boss to shove his job or sell up and move to Australia, it's not really wise to leap without thinking first as it will only add to your stress levels and put more pressure on yourself in the long run. There is nothing more depressing and de-motivating than looking at a dwindling bank account when you're desperately trying to stay focused on achieving your goals. When you are constantly reminded of your lack of money it can feel frightening, terrifying and impossible, and your goals will suffer as a result. Lack of money is undoubtedly one of the greatest things that bring people's goals to a grinding halt.

As I mentioned earlier, I clearly remember the moment when I found out how much my training was going to cost me, and momentarily I thought that was the end of my dream. But what I realised was, 'OK, so I haven't got all the money I need right now, so what. I just need to start saving every penny I've got. It might take me a little longer, but I'll get there eventually.' And this is exactly what I did. I was totally focused. I cut back on non-essential spending such as luxuries I didn't really need and set up a 'training course money pot' account and started saving everything I could each month. Within six months I had managed to claw enough money together to start my training.

You need to put together a basic financial plan of action because you need to be able to finance your goals and support yourself throughout any changes you make. Work out how much your new life is going to cost you. There is always a way around it and things are never as impossible as they first look. If you are going to need extra money to pursue your goals than make sure you add 'finances' as one of your strategies or milestones to your overall plan of action.

Exercise
Answer the following questions.

- How much money will each of your goals cost you to achieve?
- How do you plan to finance this?
- What can you do to raise the money?
- Who can help you?

Exercise
Take your most recent bank statement and go through every item systemically, marking each item listed with either '1', '2' or '3'. Number 1 indicates essential items, such as your mortgage, insurance or gas bill; basically, these are things that *must* be paid. Number 2 indicates items that aren't essential but still need paying, such as your home phone, mobile phone, food, Sky TV and so on, and, finally, number 3 indicates non-essential spending, such as meals out, clothes, hair appointments, DVDs and the like.

Once you've made this analysis, first, concentrate your efforts on items numbered '2' and '3' to see where reductions may be made. Perhaps you can change your hairdresser for someone cheaper, maybe you can change your mobile phone provider, and instead of going out for three meals a month you only do this once. Maybe now is the time to stop smoking or start making your sandwiches instead of buying them. Once you've done this, take some time to address the items numbered '1' on your statement, such as your mortgage or gas bill, and see whether there any ways you can save money by changing supplier or provider. When you look hard enough you will be able to save towards your new venture. At the end of the day it all boils down to your overall commitment: 'How much do you *really* want change in your life?' 'How much do you *really* want to achieve your goals?'

Exercise
List ten ways in which you can start saving for your new life.

Most people who decide to make big life changes have to remain in their full-time job while they retrain at weekends or in the evenings, or make some kind of sacrifice. But it's important to keep the money coming in to maintain your survival. It's only a temporary measure; it isn't forever. Be sensible and preserve your safety net. Eventually the day will come when you're finally ready to break free from your old life; you will be ready and bight-eyed to start your new one. So be patient.

What are you waiting for?

There is very little left to say other than, 'What are you waiting for?' The time has come for you to make your dreams come true. It's over to you now: your life is in your own hands. It's time to start living with more vim and vigour than ever before. It's time to stop tiptoeing around the edges of life and jump in with both feet. From this day forward commit *yourself* to taking more risks, saying 'Yes' to more opportunities and expanding your comfort zone far wider than ever before.

There is nothing holding you back now other than *you*!

A final word

You're almost there!

So you've created your life-changing goals, and you're well on your way to making the necessary changes. Your mind-set is starting to alter and those around you are beginning to see the 'new you' emerge. There's no turning back now, you've done the hard bit and you feel fantastic.

Does your evolving journey ever end? I don't honestly know as I'm still travelling. What I can tell you is, as you live your life in line with your values, talents and, ultimately, your inner spirit, your life will be blessed in ways you simply cannot imagine. Things will fall into place, life will become a breeze and people will start asking, 'What's your secret?'

But, remember, we are human beings; we are here to experience duality and we are here to experience life at both ends of the spectrum: hot and cold, light and dark, happiness and sadness, success and failure. We can't experience one without the other or life would be hideously dull. Life will sometimes throw us tough challenges, but how we deal with them is the key. The bills will still need paying, the dog will still need walking and the kids will still drive you mad. This is life. Appreciate it for what it is. See order and beauty in everything. And, when things get a little rough, let go and know that it will soon pass. What I've found is when things go wrong all your good work tends to go out of the window. As soon as you feel exposed or weak your Inner Critic will reappear from nowhere, cranking up its volume and absorbing every good thought in your head. Your old programming resurfaces and you start creating all sorts of odd behaviours and habits. When this happens it's time to stop and take time out.

I remember a few months into my newly self-employed life I went to a ladies' networking event at my local shopping centre. At the time I was frantically attending every networking or social event I could to try and attract new clients. As I sat in a circle of noisy women all trying to get their story heard I suddenly felt very vulnerable and alien to my new surroundings. I heard my Inner Critic pipe up and say 'What on earth are you doing here Louise, stop pretending and get back to your proper job!' I had spent 12 years tucked away in a nice cosy office without the need to step out of my comfort zone and there I was trying to encourage people I didn't know that they needed my services. I spent most of the morning in a world of my own waiting for the meeting to end. I just wanted to run and hide. I wanted to go home. I wanted my old, comfortable, familiar life back. In hindsight, it was just one of those days where I allowed by inner fears to take hold of me. And this will inevitably happen for you at some point. There have been numerous occasions when my goals felt colossal and far from reach, but this is normal for everyone who is committed to making big life changes. There will be times when we just want to recoil and retreat back to our old life where everything is cosy and secure – where we know where we stand. But slowly but surely, as we keep ploughing on, it gets easier and easier until the discomfort of the early days is just a distant memory. I promise it will all be worth it in the end when you look back in astonishment at the remarkable journey you have undertaken. Just keep your vision firmly locked on where it is you're going and you cannot go wrong!

No one has ever said living the life of your dreams is easy. It takes drive and determination, persistence and patience, faith and trust in the wonderful power within us, but, most importantly, it takes *action*. The greatest risk, however, comes from doing nothing at all. Life is for living not enduring!

The time has come for us to part and for you to finally let go of my hand. It's been wonderful travelling with you this far, but you are now holding everything you need to create the life you want; the life you know you deserve. When you feel a little wobbly, as we all do from time to time, remember, I'm always here, just pick up this book and keep reading until you feel strong again.

My only advice is, keep this book with you, stay focused, remain aware, connect to your inner spirit, go with the flow and most importantly enjoy the ride.

See you on the other side. You are your own fairy godmother, don't ever forget that!

Louise x

Contact Louise Presley-Turner

• For further details on workshops, talks, weekend retreats, corporate, business or one to one coaching visit www.thegameoflife.co.uk or call 01746 71 61 51

• To receive your free Game of Life newsletter log on to www.thegameoflife.co.uk

• For a 90 minute one to one Discovery Coaching Session e-mail louise@thegameoflife.co.uk

Lightning Source UK Ltd.
Milton Keynes UK
05 October 2009

144550UK00001B/3/P